"Well, WED is, you might call it my backyard laboratory, my workshop away from work."

—Walt Disney, on Walt Disney Imagineering, formerly known as WED Enterprises

The Imagineering Field Guide to the
Magic Kingdom
at Walt Disney World.

An Imagineer's-Eye Tour

By The Imagineers

EDITIONS
New York

For information address Disney Editions, 114 Fifth Avenue, New York, New York 10011–5690.

Printed in Malaysia

The following are trademarks, registered marks, and service marks owned by Disney Enterprises, Inc.: Adventureland® Area, Audio-Animatronics®, Big Thunder Mountain® Railroad, Circle-Vision, Critter Country®, Disneyland® Resort, Disneyland® Resort Paris, Disney Studios, Disney's Animal Kingdom® Park, Disney's California Adventure® Park, Epcot®, Fantasyland® Area, Frontierland® Area, Future World, Imagineering, Imagineers, "it's a small world," Magic Kingdom® Park, Main Street, U.S.A.® Area, Mickey's Toontown, monorail, New Orleans Square® Area, Space Mountain® Attraction, Splash Mountain® Attraction, Tokyo Disneyland®, Tokyo DisneySea®, Tomorrowland® Area, Toontown, Walt Disney World® Resort, World Showcase.

Buzz Lightyear's Space Ranger characters ©Disney Enterprises, Inc. and Pixar Animation Studios

TARZAN® Owned by Edgar Rice Burroughs, Inc. and Used by Permission

Winnie the Pooh characters based on the "Winnie the Pooh" works by A. A. Milne and E. H. Shepard

For Disney Editions
Editorial Director: Wendy Lefkon
Editor: Jody Revenson

Written and Designed by Alex Wright with help from all the Imagineers

For Kim, Finn, and Lincoln . . . for all that they give me, every day

The author would like to thank Jason Surrell for his example and his encouragement; Scott Otis for the use of his extensive Disney library; Jim Snyder, Greg Randle, and Jason Grandt for help with the legwork; Jody Revenson for walking a first-timer through the process; David Buckley for the use of his Sorcerer Mickey illustration on the cover; Gary Landrum for access to his SQS collections; Marty Sklar and Tom Fitzgerald for their input and for letting him do the book in the first place; Dave Smith and Robert Tieman for their thorough review; Patrick Brennan, Rhonda Counts, Ken Danberry, Tom Rodowsky, and Alex Caruthers for their park walks and stories; his parents, Peter and Paddie Wright, for bringing him to Walt Disney World so many times; and all Imagineers past and present for their assistance and for all the inspiration they've provided through the years.

Library of Congress Cataloging-in-Publication Data on file

TABLE OF CONTENTS

A Brief History of Imagineering

Walt Disney and his Imagineers at WED Enterprises, 1964

The Ultimate Workshop

Walt Disney Imagineering (WDI) is the design and development arm of The Walt Disney Company. "Imagineering" is Walt's combination of the words *imagination* and *engineering*, pointing out the combination of skills embodied by the group. Imagineers are responsible for designing and building Disney parks, resorts, cruise ships, and other entertainment venues. WDI is a highly creative organization, with a broad range of skills and talents represented. Disciplines range from writers to architects, artists to engineers, and cover all the bases in between. The Imagineers are playful, dedicated, and abundantly curious.

Walt was our first Imagineer, but as soon as he began developing the early ideas for Disneyland, he started recruiting others to help him realize his dream. He snapped up several of his most trusted and versatile animators and art directors to apply the skills of filmmaking to the three-dimensional world. They approached this task much the same as they would a film project. They wrote stories, drew storyboards, created inspirational art, assigned the production tasks to the various film-based disciplines, and built the whole thing from scratch. Disneyland is essentially a movie that allows you to walk right in and join in the fun. As Imagineer par excellence John Hench was fond of saying in response to recent trends, "Virtual reality is nothing new . . . we've been doing that for more than fifty years!"

WDI was founded on December 16, 1952, under the name WED Enterprises (from the initials **W**alter **E**lias **D**isney). Imagineering has been an integral part of the the company's culture ever since. Imagineers are the ones who ask the "what ifs?" and "why nots?" that lead to some of our most visible and most beloved landmarks. Collectively, the Disney parks have become the physical embodiment of all that our company's mythologies represent to kids of all ages.

The Dreaming Continues

Today's Imagineering is a vast and varied group, involved in projects all over the world in every stage of development, from initial conception right through to installation and even beyond that into support and constant improvement efforts. In addition to our headquarters in Glendale, California, near the company's Burbank studios, Imagineers are based at all field locations around the world. Additionally, WDI serves as a creative resource for the entire Walt Disney Company, bringing new ideas and new technologies to all of our storytellers.

Okay, Here's the Résumé

To date, Imagineers have built eleven Disney theme parks, a town, two cruise ships, dozens of resort hotels, water parks, shopping centers, sports complexes, and various entertainment venues worldwide. Some specific highlights include:

- Disneyland (1955)
- Magic Kingdom Park (1971)
- *Epcot* ® (1982)
- Tokyo Disneyland (1983)
- Disney Studios (1989)
- Typhoon Lagoon (1989)
- Pleasure Island (1989)
- Disneyland Resort Paris (1992)
- Town of Celebration (1994)

- Blizzard Beach (1995)
- Disney's Animal Kingdom Park (1998)
- DisneyQuest (1998)
- Disney Cruise Line (*Magic* 1998, *Wonder* 1999)
- ABC Times Square Studios (2000)
- Disney's California Adventure Park (2001)
- Tokyo DisneySea (2001)
- Walt Disney Studios Park (2002)
- Hong Kong Disneyland (2005)

He's on Our Name Tags

The red-robed Mickey Mouse with the blue hat, who is typically used to represent WDI, is taken from his Sorcerer's Apprentice character in the classic 1940 Disney film *Fantasia*. Sorcerer Mickey is symbolic of WDI's traditional position as the loyal group of magicmakers at the hand of Walt Disney, the ultimate wizard. It's worth noting that the sorcerer in *Fantasia* was named Yensid, or the name "Disney" spelled backward.

ALEX

7

WDI Disciplines

Imagineers form a diverse organization, with over 140 different job titles working toward the common goal of telling great stories. WDI has an exceptionally broad collection of disciplines considering its size, due to the highly specialized nature of our work. In everything it does, WDI is supported by many other divisions of The Walt Disney Company.

Tiki Room concept by John Hench

Show/Concept Design and Illustration produces the early drawings and renderings that serve as the inspiration for our projects and provides us with the initial visual communication. This artwork gives the entire team a shared vision.

Show Writing develops the stories we want to tell in the parks, as well as any nomenclature that is required. This group writes the scripts for our attractions, the copy for plaques, and names our lands, rides, shops, vehicles, and restaurants.

Adventureland facade elevation by Rabey

Architecture is responsible for turning those fanciful show drawings into real buildings, meeting all of the functional requirements that are expected of them. Our parks present some unique architectural challenges.

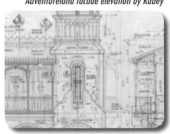

Interior Designers are responsibile for the design details of the inside of our buildings. They develop the look and feel of interior spaces and select finishes, furniture, and fixtures to complete the design.

Engineering determines all of our mechanical standards and figures out how to make our ideas work. Engineers verify structures and systems for buildings, bridges, rides, and play spaces, and solve the tricky problems we throw their way every day.

Lighting Design puts all the hard work the rest of us have done on our shows and attractions into the best light. Lighting designers are also responsible for specifying all of the themed lighting fixtures found in the parks. As our lighting designers are fond of telling us, "without lights, it's radio!"

Adventureland graphic by Bob McDonnell

Graphic Designers produce signage, both flat and dimensional, in addition to providing lots of the artwork, patterns, and details that finish the Disney show. Marquees and directional signs are just a couple of examples of their work.

Prop Design is concerned with who "lives" in a given area of a park. All of the pieces and parts of everyday life that tell you about a person or a location are very carefully selected and placed. These props have to be found, purchased, prepped, built, and installed.

Sound Designers work to develop the auditory backdrop for everything you see and experience. Sound is one of the most evocative senses. The songs in the attractions, the background music in the lands, and the sound effects built into show elements all work together to complete our illusions.

Media Design creates all of the various film, video, audio, and onscreen interactive content in our parks. Our Theme Park Productions unit (TPP) serves as something of an in-house production studio for WDI.

9

Landscape Architecture is the discipline that focuses on our plant palette and area development. This includes the layout of all of our hardscape and the arrangement of foliage elements on and between attractions.

Show Set Design takes concepts and breaks them down into bite-size pieces that are organized into drawing and drafting packages, integrated into the architectural, mechanical, civil, or other components of the project, and tracked during fabrication.

Show set design by Thom Flowers

Character Paint creates the reproductions of various materials, finishes, and states of aging whenever we need to make something new look old.

Character Plaster produces the hard finishes in the Park that mimic other materials. This includes rockwork, themed paving, and architectural facades such as faux stone and plaster. They even use concrete to imitate wood!

Dimensional Design is the art of modelmaking. This skill is used to work out various design issues ahead of time in model form, ensuring that our relative scales and spatial relationships are properly coordinated. Models are a wonderful tool for problem-solving.

Fabrication Design involves developing and implementing the production strategies that allow us to build all the specialized items on the large and complex projects that we deliver. Somebody has to figure out how to build the impossible!

Special Effects creates all of the magical (but also totally believable) smoke, fire, lightning, ghosts, explosions, pixie dust, wind, rain, snow, and sparks that give our stories action and a sense of surprise. Some of these effects are quite simple, while others rely on the most sophisticated technologies that can be drawn from the field of entertainment or any other imaginable industry.

Production Design starts with the show design, takes it to the next level of detail, and ensures that it can be built so as to maintain the creative intent. It also has the task of integrating the show with all the other systems that will need to be coordinated in the field during installation.

Master Planning looks into the future and maps out the best course of action for laying out all of our properties for development. In fact, they see farther into the future than any other Imagineering division, often working with an eye toward projects that might be decades away from realization.

R&D stands for Research & Development. WDI R&D is the group that gets to play with the coolest toys. They investigate and invent all the latest technologies from every field of study and look for ways to apply them to Disney entertainment. WDI R&D serves as a resource for the entire Walt Disney Company.

Project Management is responsible for organizing our teams, our schedules, and our processes so that our projects can be delivered when they're supposed to be and at the expected level of quality.

Construction Management oversees our building efforts in the field. They ensure that every job meets the Disney construction standards, including quality control, code compliance, and long-term durability during operation.

Imagineering Lingo

WDI has a very vibrant and unique culture, which is even embodied in the terms we throw around the office when we're working. Here is a guide to help you understand us a bit better as we show you around the Park.

Area Development - The interstitial spaces between the attractions, restaurants, and shops. This would include landscape architecture, propping, show elements, and special enhancements intended to expand the experience.

Audio-Animatronics - The term for the three-dimensional animated actors of all species we employ to perform in our shows and attractions. Audio-Animatronics was invented by Imagineers at Walt's request, and is an essential piece in the process in the development of many iconic Disney attractions.

Berm - A raised earthen barrier, typically heavily landscaped, which serves to eliminate visual intrusions into the Park from the outside world and block the outside world from intruding inside.

BGM - Background Music. The musical selections that fill in the audio landscape as you make your way around the Park. Each BGM track is carefully selected, arranged, and recorded to enhance the story being told.

Blue Sky - The early stages in the idea generation process when anything is possible. There are not yet any considerations taken into account that might reign in the creative process. At this point, the sky's the limit!

Brainstorm - A gathering for the purpose of generating as many ideas as possible in the shortest time possible. We hold many brainstorming sessions at WDI, always looking for the best ideas. Imagineering has a set of Brainstorming Rules, which are always adhered to.

> **Rule 1-** There is no such thing as a bad idea. We never know how one idea (however far-fetched) might lead into another one that is exactly right.
> **Rule 2-** We don't talk yet about *why not*. There will be plenty of time for realities later, so we don't want them to get in the way of the good ideas now.
> **Rule 3-** Nothing should stifle the flow of ideas. No buts or can'ts, or other "stopping" words. We want to hear words such as "and," "or," and "what if?"
> **Rule 4-** There is no such thing as a bad idea. (We take that one very seriously.)

Charrette - Another term for a brainstorming session. From the French word for "cart." It refers to the cart sent through the Latin Quarter in Paris to collect the art and design projects of students at the legendary École des Beaux-Arts who were unable to deliver them to the school themselves after the mad rush to complete their work at the end of the term.

Concept - An idea and the effort put into communicating it and developing it into something usable. A concept can be expressed as a drawing, a written description, or simply a verbal pitch. Everything we do starts out as a concept.

Dark Ride - A term often used to describe the charming little Fantasyland attractions housed more or less completely inside a show building, which allows for greater isolation of show elements and light control, as needed.

Elevation - A drawing of a true frontal view of an object, often drawn from multiple sides, eliminating the perspective that you would see in the real world, for clarity in the design and to lead construction activities.

E-Ticket - The top level of attractions. This dates back to an early Disneyland ticketing system used to distribute ridership through all attractions in the Park. Each was assigned a letter (A,B,C,D,E) indicating where it fell in the Park's pecking order.

Kinetics – Movement and motion in a scene that give it life and energy. This can come from moving vehicles, active signage, changes in the lighting, special effects, or even hanging banners or flags that move around as the wind blows.

Maquette – A model, especially a sculpture, depicting a show element in miniature scale so that design issues can be worked out before construction begins. It's much easier to make changes on a maquette than on a full-size anything.

Plan – A direct overhead view of an object or a space. Very useful in verifying relative sizes of elements and the flow of Guests and show elements through an area.

Plussing – A word derived from Walt's penchant for always trying to make an idea better. Imagineers are continually trying to *plus* their work, even after it's "finished."

POV – Point Of View. The position from which something is seen, or the place an artist chooses to use as the vantage point of the imaginary viewer in a concept illustration. POVs are chosen in order to best represent the idea being shown.

Propping – The placement of objects around a scene. From books on a shelf to place settings on a table to wall hangings in an office space, props are the elements that give a set life and describe the people who live there. They are the everyday objects we see all around but that point out so much about us if you pay attention to them.

Section – A drawing that looks as if it's a slice through an object or space. This is very helpful in seeing how various elements interrelate. It is typically drawn as though it were an elevation, with heavier line weights defining where our imaginary cut would be.

Show – Everything we put "onstage" in a Disney park. Walt believed that everything we put out for the Guests in our parks was part of a big show, so much of our terminology originated in the show business world. With that in mind, *show* becomes for us a very broad term that includes just about anything our Guests see, hear, smell, or come in contact with during their visit to any of our Parks or Resorts.

Story – Story is the fundamental building block of everything WDI does. Imagineers are, above all, storytellers. The time, place, characters, and plot points that give our work meaning start with the story, which is also the framework that guides all design decisions.

Storyboard – A large pin-up board used to post ideas in a charrette or to outline the story points of a ride or film. The technique was perfected by Walt in the early days of his animation studio and became a staple of the animated film development process. The practice naturally transferred over to WDI when so many of the early Imagineers came over from Walt's Animation department.

Theme – The fundamental nature of a story in terms of what it means to us, or the choice of time, place, and decor applied to an area in order to support that story.

THRC – Theoretical Hourly Ride Capacity. The number of guests per hour that can experience an attraction under optimal conditions. THRC is always taken into account when a new attraction is under consideration.

Visual Intrusion – Any outside element that makes its way into a scene, breaks the visual continuity, and destroys the illusion. WDI works hard to eliminate visual intrusions.

Weenie – Walt's playful term for a visual element that could be used to draw people into and around a space. A weenie is big enough to be seen from a distance and interesting enough to make you want to take a closer look, like Cinderella Castle at the end of Main Street, U.S.A., or the Astro Orbiter in Tomorrowland. Weenies are critical to our efforts at laying out a sequence of story points in an organized fashion.

MAGIC KINGDOM PARK

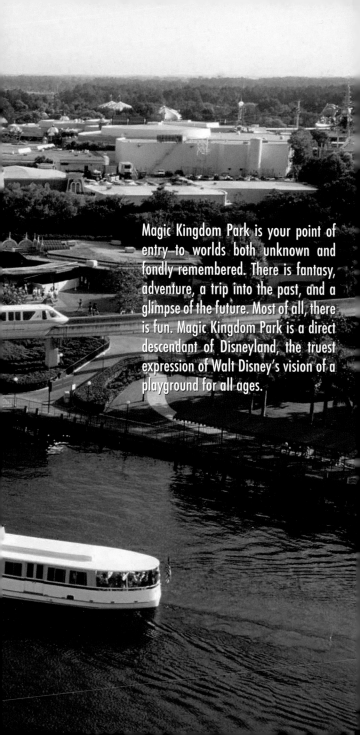

Magic Kingdom Park is your point of entry to worlds both unknown and fondly remembered. There is fantasy, adventure, a trip into the past, and a glimpse of the future. Most of all, there is fun. Magic Kingdom Park is a direct descendant of Disneyland, the truest expression of Walt Disney's vision of a playground for all ages.

Disneyland East

They're Inseparable!

You can't tell the story of Magic Kingdom Park without talking about Disneyland. Though distinct entities with their own individual identities, the two share a common origin and an intertwining history. Many of the attractions found at Walt Disney World are shared with Disneyland and the other Disneyland-style parks the Imagineers have built since. You will hear many references to Disneyland throughout this book.

July 17, 1955, saw the birth of a brand new benchmark in family entertainment. Disneyland opened its gates to the world and changed our perceptions of fantasy and reality, the possible and the impossible, and even our definition of family fun itself. Walt Disney's vision of a playground for families and children of all ages was evidently shared by many, and the Park has been going strong ever since.

However, Walt wasn't the type to rest on his laurels. He was always looking for the next thing to do—bigger and better than anything he had done before. Walt Disney World (WDW) was his next big thing. By all accounts, it was the ideas for "The Florida Project" that consumed much of his thought over the course of his final years.

A key milestone in its gestation was the 1964-1965 New York World's Fair. Walt and his Imagineers developed shows for four of the pavilions at the Fair, for clients as diverse as UNICEF, Ford Motor Company, General Electric, and the State of Illinois. This was the first test of whether the Disneyland concept would find favor on the East Coast. Prior to this event, there was some concern that it would not work outside the fantasy world of Hollywood and Southern California.

Walt had grown frustrated over his inability to control or even influence what was built right outside the boundaries of the Disneyland property in Anaheim. He felt that it cluttered and diluted what he was trying to achieve with that park, and he was determined not to make the same mistake again—and in Florida, he didn't.

The Walt Disney World project was begun in earnest around 1965, when the Company began buying up thousands of acres of swamp and pasture land in Central Florida near Orlando. The location was critical to Walt, as its proximity to major highways, existing tourist destinations, and a growing regional airport made it ideal to lure and distribute the crowds he hoped to entertain. The weather in the region was also thought to be ideal, allowing for year-round operation of the Park and a broad range of outdoor recreational activities, making for a very well-rounded Guest experience.

The land was purchased under assumed names so as not to attract attention—Walt did not yet want anybody to know what he was up to. This effort is commemorated with a special window on Main Street. The land purchase totalled 27,258 acres at a cost of just over $5 million. Once the land had been acquired, it was on to phase two.

This land was (and is) roughly twice the size of Manhattan, or about the same area as the city of San Francisco. The development effort would be, at its peak, the largest private construction project in the United States. The intent was to capture the magic of Disneyland while developing a significant vacation destination. The property, thought by many to be undevelopable, presented its own set of challenges—compounded by the very high standards set out by the project team. The effort was intended to serve as a model for efficiency and environmental responsibility in urban planning for the rest of the world to follow. No small task, to be sure.

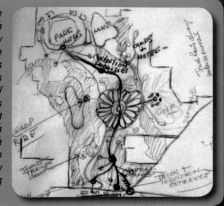

This amazingly accurate master planning sketch was drawn in 1965 by Walt Disney himself as he began to form the ideas that would lead the efforts in Florida. Walt saw WDW as a city planning effort as much as an entertainment enterprise. He put much thought into how each element would relate to the rest of the property and to the surrounding environment.

Complicating matters was the fact that Walt Disney died in December 1966, before construction had begun. The Company had lost its leader and visionary, and even with the best intentions of those left to carry on his dream, there was uncertainty over whether the project would proceed. This uncertainty didn't last long, however, as Walt's older brother, Roy, quickly stepped up to ensure its completion. Roy had been Walt's business partner for forty-three years and was the perfect financial and planning counterpoint to Walt's flights of fanciful imagination. Now Roy took the forefront, postponing his impending retirement to see that his brother's greatest dream did not die with him. He even insisted on changing the name of the resort, adding the *Walt* to the previously planned *Disney World* so that there would be no doubt whose vision was being realized.

Like Disneyland, but Different

Walt Disney reveals his intentions for The Florida Project in 1965.

We Never Repeat Ourselves, We Never Repeat Ourselves

Though Magic Kingdom Park owes its existence to Disneyland and is drawn from the same central ideas, there are significant differences between the two parks. Some represent lessons gleaned during the construction and early operation of Disneyland. Others are the result of creative variations introduced by the designers, and new film properties produced by the Studio. Still others are merely reflective of the time of their development. It was always important to Walt that the two parks have their own identities. He did not care to repeat himself, so for the Florida park to be a mirror image of the original would have been seen by him as a failing. To that end, Imagineers have continued to develop the two parks independently, so they would continue to provide two very different experiences—both worthy of the Disney name.

Both parks feature a train around the perimeter, a castle in the middle, Main Street, U.S.A., Fantasyland, Frontierland, Adventureland, and Tomorrowland. Even these demonstrate variations both major and minor. Disneyland features two lands adjacent to its Frontierland—Critter Country and New Orleans Square. Magic Kingdom Park does not, but adds Liberty Square—originally conceived as an extension of Main Street at Disneyland. And the Florida version of Toontown is more of a small town than a bustling 'toon metropolis.

Magic Kingdom Park is bigger than Disneyland, covering approximately 120 acres compared to 80 acres at Disneyland. Also, Disneyland was developed solely as an entertainment enterprise. The master plan for Walt Disney World was far more ambitious, as Walt's visions of a precisely designed community took shape. These goals led to the most distinct variations between the two parks, and make WDW a uniquely interesting effort in urban planning.

Right This Way, Please

Looking at Disneyland through the eyes of a filmmaker, and working as he always did to make constant improvements based on lessons learned, Walt had a few new things in mind for Magic Kingdom Park. Among these was a wish to create a better introduction to the show so as not to throw the Guests too quickly into the story without giving them a chance to separate themselves from the outside world. The "blessing of size," as he called it, afforded him this opportunity.

The location of the Magic Kingdom on the WDW property was chosen with this in mind. An area of natural swampland near the north end of the site was deemed a prime candidate to be fashioned into a body of water around which to place resort hotels and on which to offer water sports and other recreational activities. Placing the Park on one side and the parking lot on the other gave Walt the sense of arrival he was seeking.

Walt's cinematic eye informed everything he did with his parks.

Think about the way you, as a typical Guest, approach and enter the Park. From the Transportation and Ticket Center, where most Guests have left their cars, Cinderella Castle is visible. This heightens the feeling of anticipation one is already experiencing. Once you board the monorail or ferry, you know you're on your way and you get caught up in the excitement of the journey. You get periodic glimpses of the Castle, but it's not generally in plain sight. Upon arrival at the Park entrance (our theater lobby), the height of the train station serves as a visual barrier to the Park. The music here is chosen to represent all the lands of the Park, orchestrated so as not to clash with the visible elements of Main Street. You pass through tunnels where your view is constricted, and it gets darker before the first reveal of Town Square. The pass-throughs are placed on opposite sides of the Square, so that you can't initially see all the way down the street. Once you've had a chance to get your bearings and soak in the atmosphere of Main Street, you're funneled toward the center of the street where the Castle is finally given away in the ultimate reveal. It's all intentional, and highly cinematic—by design, of course.

MAIN STREET, U.S.A.

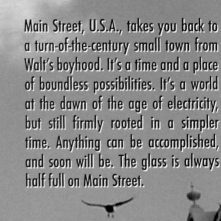

Main Street, U.S.A., takes you back to a turn-of-the-century small town from Walt's boyhood. It's a time and a place of boundless possibilities. It's a world at the dawn of the age of electricity, but still firmly rooted in a simpler time. Anything can be accomplished, and soon will be. The glass is always half full on Main Street.

That Hometown Feeling

Town Square concept by Dorothea Redmond

Main Street, U.S.A., is the perfect way to start a day at the Magic Kingdom. It's a trip back to a time and place we all "remember," though few of us—especially today—have actually ever been there. It is the dawn of the Industrial Revolution at the advent of electricity. Horseless carriages share the road with horse-drawn trollies. Gas lamps are being replaced by electric bulbs. The place is all hustle and bustle.

Walt wanted Main Street to embody the American spirit. It is a place where people are friendly, hard work is rewarded, and everybody shares a dream for a better life. This is representative of Walt's heartfelt patriotism and love for his country and is part of the message he always wanted to convey with his work.

Building elevation by Ernie Prinzhorn

Main Street in Magic Kingdom Park is much bigger than Main Street at Disneyland, in keeping with the general upsizing of the entire Park and its taller Castle. It is the Main Street of a slightly larger burgeoning town. There are more signs of industrialization, and the architecture is slightly more ornate, in a style we call "Eastern seaboard Victorian." This style came into vogue during the 1880s and 1890s as the Industrial Revolution made possible the mass fabrication of precut architectural details that could be shipped around the country. The lighter and lacier metalwork lends Main Street a more fanciful flair to illustrate the overriding optimism.

Reality vs Memories

Main Street, U.S.A., at Disneyland is based on Walt's recollections of his childhood home of Marceline, Missouri, though by all accounts it is more closely tied to his *memories* of Marceline than the reality of what Marceline was at the time. This is an example of heightened reality, a design technique used to invoke feelings of nostalgia, whether historically accurate or not. Heightened reality is a staple of the Imagineering toolbox, giving us the artistic license to play more directly to our emotional attachments to design details rather than to strict adherence to historical accuracy.

Even more than Marceline, Main Street at Disneyland probably looks like Ft. Collins, Colorado, the hometown of art director Harper Goff, who did many of the initial drawings of the land. This early drawing shows Harper's interpretation of those memories.

Heightened reality can be observed elsewhere in the Park, as well. The Western locale of our Frontierland is an idealized version of real pioneer towns. Adventureland is a romanticized expression of the tropical locales it represents. Tomorrowland is a fantastical vision of a world of the future that *probably* will never exist in exactly that form. And Fantasyland combines hints of real-world architecture with exaggerated details, then heaps on excess levels of charm to depict the Medieval carnival, the Alpine village, and the English Tudor style we've always imagined in our storybooks. All of these examples rely on the same formula—take the things people "know" from the world around them, select the ones that suit the story you wish to tell, and combine them into something that is entirely new but that still feels oddly familiar.

A Different Perspective, Entirely

Main Street, U.S.A., provides the perfect backdrop for a discussion of forced perspective—a theatrical design technique whereby the designer plays with scale in the real world in order to affect the perception of scale in an illusory world. We all carry with us a sixth-sense understanding of relative scale, and it is that familiarity that allows Imagineers to trick us by changing the "rules." Buildings, props, or set pieces are built with size relationships that might be incorrect in order to increase the apparent size or distance of an object or space.

Forced perspective can be found around all the Disney parks. It is found in large exterior spaces and in smaller interior sets and models. It's just another way in which the world you encounter here at the Park might not be exactly as it appears. Some of the most often cited examples of forced perspective are found right here on Main Street. For example, each building, with few exceptions, is built with floors that diminish in height in an effort to make them appear taller than they really are without making the whole of Main Street too large and impersonal. One exception is Town Square Exposition Hall, which was built full size in order to mitigate the potential visual intrusion from Disney's Contemporary Resort off to the south and east of the Park. Also, the train station is necessarily full scale, as the upper floor is actually used by Guests. This also serves the function of obscuring the view into the Park toward the Castle until we wish to reveal it.

Cinderella Castle, seen at the end of Main Street, is the most extreme example of this practice. The scale of the architectural elements and building blocks is significantly different in the upper reaches than in the lower foundation in order to make the Castle seem to soar beyond its 189-foot actual height. The stacked stones of the lower castle walls get smaller and smaller in size as you scan upward. In fact, the handrail at the top spire, where Tinker Bell begins her flight before the fireworks, is only two feet tall rather than the three-and-a-half-foot-tall railings we're used to seeing in standard construction.

This forced perspective, combined with the depth of the hub beyond the end of the street, opens up a vast and exhilarating vista to the Guest entering the Park for a day of adventure. Conversely, the full-size buildings around Town Square and the lesser depth of the Square itself conspire to make the same path appear shorter to that same weary Guest trudging toward the exit at the end of the day. Think of it as an optical illusion for your feet.

Third story 8 feet

Second story 10 feet

First story 12 feet

This diagram demonstrates the principle of forced perspective as applied to the Plaza Ice Cream Parlor on Main Street, U.S.A. Each floor is a bit smaller than the floor below, making a three-story building a bit more comfortable in scale.

A Window to the Past

One of the most treasured traditions within the Disney Company is the honor of having one's name placed on a window on Main Street. For the Disney theme-park historian, the windows serve as a fascinating look into the background of the people who have made the magic happen. The folks represented on these windows come from many different areas of the Company. There are Imagineers, operators, developers, corporate officers, artisans, and more. The common thread is that they are all credited with making a significant impact on the Magic Kingdom and the legacy of Disney Parks.

Each window is carefully designed, the way any other element in the Park would be. The imaginary profession of the new resident of Main Street is typically chosen to relate to the activities of the real-world counterpart on which he or she is based. Some of the cleverest turns of a phrase in all of Disney Park nomenclature can be found here. The graphic layout is handled by one of our designers, and the honoree receives a scale-model replica at a ceremony held on Main Street, at which the real window is revealed.

First in Line

Fittingly, the very first window on Main Street, U.S.A., visible from outside the Park, is dedicated to Walt Disney. This one pays homage to his love of trains, and designates him as the "Chief Engineer" for the Walt Disney World Railroad. This is the first of his two prominent windows. If you look closely at the windows over the Plaza Restaurant at the other end of Main Street, you'll see a window marked simply "Walt Disney, Master Classes in Design and Master Planning." This one, along with the first window placed on the face of the train station, helps to bookend our "credits," with the director listed first and last, much like a typical film title sequence. So, pay attention to these and others along Main Street, U.S.A. There's a story, and a talented and dedicated person, behind each and every one of them. Try to figure out who or what the story might be, just by window-hopping.

Higher and Higher

Former Disney President and Chief Operating Officer Frank Wells's window pays homage to his fondness for mountain climbing. His window for Seven Summits Expeditions is located on the third floor of the Main Street Market House, higher than any other window on the street—just one more peak surmounted by Frank.

QUICK TAKES

• M. T. Lott Real Estate Investments—This is a collection of pseudonymous companies used by Disney to secretly buy all of the land that would become Walt Disney World, and the Company executive, Donn Tatum, who led the effort. The team didn't want the public to know who was doing the purchasing or why they wanted that big, empty lot.

• The Center Street Academy of Fine Art—This window pays tribute to some of the greatest fine artists ever to work for Disney and WDI, including Mary Blair, Herb Ryman, Blaine Gibson, and John Hench.

• Hollywood Publishing—The lead Show Writers for the Magic Kingdom project are recognized by this entry: F. X. Atencio, Al Bertino, and Marty Sklar. Their words are found throughout the Park, so it's only fitting that they are put into words here.

These windows recognize various company luminaries such as former Disney CEO Card Walker; Yale Gracey, Bud Martin, Ken O'Brien, and Wathel Rogers of WDI Special Effects; and Ub & Don Iwerks for their work in camera optics.

"A" Ticket to Ride

Part of the atmosphere of any time or place is the style of the vehicles that move people about. This can go a long way toward selling the viewer on the environment and ambience of any sort of imaginary setting. Our vehicles are one of the most direct reflections of our level of technology, the density of our population, and our activity level. Is the city bustling? Is the town booming? Is the rural area industrialized? All of these questions can typically be answered with a quick glance at the local transportation systems.

Much of the charm of Main Street, U.S.A., comes from the assortment of vehicles that share the street with the pedestrians. It's the classic juxtaposition of the horseless carriage and the horse-drawn trolley that tells you instantly just what time you're in and what sort of place it is. Walt always insisted that the vehicles be onstage and accurate. Imagineer Tony Baxter tells the story of how Walt used to come into Disneyland in the morning prior to opening so that he could drive the Carnation milk truck around on Main Street.

We have the trolleys, we have the jitneys (old-fashioned automobiles of various vintages), and we have the ever-popular fire engine. In the early days, when ticket books were still in effect, the vehicles on Main Street tended to be A-Tickets. They were simple little activities, and a means of traveling from one end of the street to the other in a way that immersed you in the story. Just having them around on the street makes for a more complete and convincing environment—one that feels lived-in and alive.

The Main Street Fire Engine—a longtime favorite

A horse-drawn trolley waits for a fare at the Central Plaza.

Catch a Ride

The Main Street fleet of horseless carriages are replicas based on composites of various Franklin Automobile models of the 1903–1907 era that run on four-cylinder Hercules gasoline engines. It turns out it's tough to keep actual 100-year-old cars running all day, each and every day! Oversight of this type of specialty manufacturing typically falls under WDI's watch.

Fire Engine design by Bob Gurr

The cumulative effect of all this commotion is to reinforce the notion that this is an exciting place bristling with energy. All of these vehicles offer a great tour of Main Street, a chance to rest your feet, and a lift from here to there. The drivers all know this town like the back of their hand, so they're always excellent sources of information. Whether you're here for the first time or the hundred and first, these vehicles help to make your visit to our little town pleasant and immersive.

29

Business Is Booming

The Emporium is the home of the busiest commerce on Main Street. This shop—established in 1901 just like Walt—was designed to demonstrate the period department store of such a town. Our Emporium has even been designed to illustrate the success of the imaginary proprietor. Even though this character has never been designed nor seen in the Parks, his Imagineered story line is used to guide our design development. When the Emporium expanded into Center Street in 2002, the wealth and travels of this owner were put on display. The original Victorian space has always shown signs of opulence in the finishes and the fixturing, such as the combination gas and electric chandeliers—the electric lamps point down, the gas lamps point up—a tremendous extravagance during this era. The expansion revealed the ways the proprietor has been spending his money. The architecture is intended to reflect influences brought back a few years later, circa 1903, from Europe, revealed in its Edwardian style. This shows itself through the lighter woods and pastel color scheme, contrasting with the heavier woods and reddish tones of the pre-existing space. This project explains our reliance on story to guide design. Until the story is finalized, it can be anything, but once we set our rules through that story, we stick by them. It helps us make our choices and gives us something to build onto.

Concept rendering for the Emporium expansion by Joe Warren

Where's the Fire?

As you enter Town Square, don't rush by the red brick building on the left side. That firehouse is an important piece of the fabric of Main Street. Every small town has a fire station, and ours is no exception. The Fire Station at Disneyland was built with an apartment to be used by the Disney family, which is still there to this day. The Disney apartment at WDW was to have been placed inside Cinderella Castle.

The Engine Co. 71 sign over the row of second-story windows refers to the fact that Magic Kingdom Park opened in 1971.

The propping inside—a mix of real and fabricated pieces—is quite extensive, going a long way toward making you believe that people actually live and work there. The work bays at the rear, particularly, devote a great deal of space to this effort.

A longtime tradition at the Park is that of the placement of various fire department insignia in the Main Street Fire Station. Firefighters from around the country bring their patches with them to leave behind or mail them in after their visits to show their stations' colors for all to see.

31

Partners, Indeed

The Walt and Roy statues on Main Street

The Walt and Mickey *Partners* statue in the Central Plaza and the Roy and Minnie statue in Town Square are significant landmarks. Both were sculpted by Blaine Gibson, but many Imagineers who knew and worked with the two Disneys were consulted. There was much thought put into the specifics of each pairing and all of the poses. Walt is rendered as the visionary, in a hero's stance, pointing toward the future and leading the way for his creation, Mickey Mouse. Roy is presented in a more modest posture, sitting on a bench looking rather unassuming and even supporting the hand of Minnie Mouse, who has approached him to make contact. Roy's statue is intended to recognize his willingness to remain somewhat in the background while working so hard to realize Walt's visions.

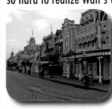

I'm Ready for my Close-up, Mr. D.

Main Street is one of the best places to scout examples of the WDI practice of designing for close, medium, and long shots, articulated so well over the years by Imagineer John Hench. The idea is that long views establish an idea, medium views continue to support the idea, and close-ups don't provide any elements that contradict it. This is why we pay so much attention to details such as carpet patterns, doorknobs, lighting fixtures, and furniture. If you keep the story in mind as you select these elements and coordinate well with a design that's already been completed for a given scene, it allows for a consistency of thought, even with projects as large and as collaborative as ours.

Who? What? When? Where? Why?

Many of our design disciplines serve to answer these questions, but Prop Design gives the real sense of life to a space. The props tell us so much about *when* this is, *who* lives here, and *what* they do. A space without propping feels vacant and uninteresting. If we don't believe that anyone lives here, it's hard to feel caught up in their story. Main Street, U.S.A., features several examples of great propping, shown here in the Main Street Athletic Club and the Car Barn.

QUICK TAKES

• Walt wanted the storefront windows on Main Street to be placed closer to the ground than would be period-correct so that children would be able to see inside.

• The bright red of the sidewalks in Town Square and in the hub area was chosen to enhance the green of the grass, as the two colors are opposites on the color wheel.

• The attraction posters that hang in the Train Station, illustrating the stories and adventures that await as you enter the Park, are part of our attempt to set the scene for the arriving Guest.

• The "Tony" of Tony's Town Square Restaurant—whose facade was influenced by the Hotel Saratoga in New York—is the Italian chef who serves spaghetti to the title characters in the film *Lady and the Tramp*. Be careful not to step on the monument to their love carved into the pavement in front of the entry. It's paws-atively adorable.

• The music is, of course, chosen to represent the period, but also to evoke a sense of optimism with a fanfare of upbeat, bouncy tempos.

• The buffer zones of landscaping placed around the hub are used as part of the transition from Main Street to the other lands of the Park.

• Many of the windows over Main Street are lit from behind with flicker lamps, and some even have special effects that cast shadows to make the street continue to feel occupied after dark.

Ridin' the Rails

Walt Disney checking the workings of the original Lilly Belle

You can't properly tell the story of Disneyland, or of Magic Kingdom Park for that matter, without talking about trains. Walt's love of trains, and the shared fascination he found with several of his animators at the Studio, forms one of the essential building blocks of Walt's parks. All of the early iterations of what would eventually become Disneyland, including some initial plans for the little Riverside park at the Disney Studio lot in Burbank, prominently featured a train as a means of providing transportation, setting the scene, and telling the story.

Walt always carried with him a fondness for trains, so when he learned of the railroad hobbies, model and otherwise, of some of his artists, it piqued his interest. Ollie Johnston and Ward Kimball, two of his Nine Old Men of animation, were quite serious hobbyists. Ward even had a full-size train set up in his backyard! Before long, Walt chose the site for his family home specifically so that he would have room for a miniature train setup of his own, and enlisted Roger Broggie and Wathel Rogers from the Studio machine shop to help him build it. These two future Imagineers, known for their mechanical skills, assisted in the fabrication of the Carolwood–Pacific railway line (referring to the Carolwood Drive address of the house in Holmby Hills), a true one-eighth scale replica of a locomotive engine from the late 1800s. He named it the *Lilly Belle*, after his wife, Lillian. Walt set up an elaborate track throughout the entire yard, where he gave rides to celebrities, friends, and lots of kids, at speeds of up to 30 mph. He even came upon the idea of the berm during the development of this layout, as he had placed an earthen barrier around his property so as not to bother the neighbors with the noise from his train!

The locomotives of the WDW Railroad are the *Lilly Belle*, the *Walter E. Disney*, the *Roy O. Disney*, and the *Roger E. Broggie*. Each name is placed on the side of the conductor's cabin. There are plaques relating the story of each of these folks placed in the station's central lobby. All four of them were, of course, essential to the existence of Disneyland and, by extension, that of the Magic Kingdom.

The four locomotives date from 1916 to 1928 and were built by the Baldwin Locomotive Works of Philadelphia, Pennsylvania. After being salvaged from the Yucatan Peninsula in Mexico, they were shipped to the Tampa Shipbuilding and Dry Dock Company for restoration. At this time all of the tenders and coaches were built from scratch.

The name of one of the first Imagineers on the cab of the Roger E. Broggie

DEPARTING TRAINS

RKS

YED

TRACK | KIMBALL CANYON

REM

An appreciative homage to animator Ward Kimball, from the Imagineers

The vast majority of the propping in the Main Street Station has been carefully chosen and placed to further the story of a turn-of-the-century small-town railway depot, or to explain the connection between Walt, the Disney parks, and trains. There are carts and arcade games, informational plaques and historical photos. There is, however, one especially playful touch. Perched on a shelf in the lobby—shown below—is a collection of passenger luggage for patrons waiting to board. See if you can guess which land each is headed for.

ADVENTURELAND

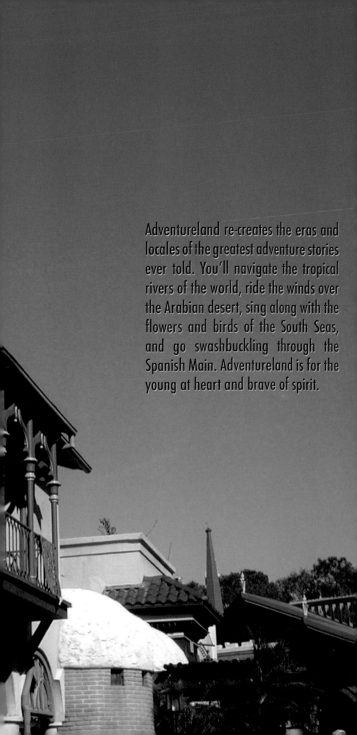

Adventureland re-creates the eras and locales of the greatest adventure stories ever told. You'll navigate the tropical rivers of the world, ride the winds over the Arabian desert, sing along with the flowers and birds of the South Seas, and go swashbuckling through the Spanish Main. Adventureland is for the young at heart and brave of spirit.

Setting the Scene

Bird's-eye view of the Jungle Cruise load area in Disneyland by Sam McKim

What Does "Adventure" Look Like?

It's a good question, isn't it? *Adventure* is a very broad term that brings to mind a very broad range of images. For some, it can be a time, for others a place. For others still, it has more to do with a spirit or a state of mind. So, how do you create a place that looks like adventure to *everyone*? Figuring that out was one of the first tasks handed by Walt to his Imagineers.

Since many disparate images come to mind when one hears the word "Adventure," our Adventureland intentionally plays on several of these themes and settings. There are the deep, dark jungles of Africa, the islands of the Caribbean Sea, the South Seas tropics, and an Arabian bazaar. It is the combination of all of these locales that creates an overall sense of adventure to serve as a backdrop for the stories we want to tell.

The *Disneyland* television show, which served as Walt's introduction of the Park to his future Guests, began each segment with a brief introduction that linked that evening's presentation to one of the lands he had planned for Disneyland, and many offered a progress report on the Park under construction. The stories on which the Park was based in the first place were now put to use to explain the new Park to others. There were Davy Crockett episodes for Frontierland, tales of space travel for Tomorrowland, and cartoons for Fantasyland. These, along with the *True-Life Adventure* series of documentary films, served notice as to what Walt had in mind for his Park and with this land. As a matter of fact, in the early planning stages for Disneyland, Adventureland was referred to by the working title True-Life Adventureland.

From Here to There

The Crystal Palace transitions Main Street, U.S.A., into Adventureland. Its architecture was based on a combination of sources—the San Francisco Conservatory of Flowers, Kew Gardens in England, and the Crystal Palace in New York. Elements from these varying sources were combined into a particularly Victorian edifice in order to serve as the gateway to the Colonial-inspired visions of Africa and Asia that form the basis of the architecture of Adventureland nearest the hub.

Adventureland entry concepts by Dorothea Redmond and Herb Ryman

These concepts demonstrate the variety of approaches one can take with this land.

Ready, Set, Design!

Jungle Cruise elevation by Harper Goff

Harper Goff, one of the first Imagineers brought on board by Walt—straight from his work on the Disney film *20,000 Leagues Under the Sea*—left his stamp all over Disneyland. His designs were particularly influential in the flavor and charm of Main Street, U.S.A., and in the character and mystery of Adventureland. His broad experience as a motion picture art director made him a perfect choice to render and produce Walt's ambitious visions in three dimensions.

Jungle Cruise

Animal Adventures

Temple ruin concept by Marc Davis

Jungle Cruise was one of the first early attractions not based on a Disney animated film. On the suggestion of Harper Goff, the attraction took its inspiration from the film *The African Queen*. Walt's early plans for the Jungle Cruise included real live animals. Inspired by the success of his *True-Life Adventure* films, he was determined to bring these wonders of nature to a place where Guests could see them up close and share his admiration. Upon consultation with animal-care specialists, Walt was convinced that although the domesticated mules and horses in Frontierland could generally be counted on to perform their roles, live exotic animals would never provide the consistent show he wanted. They couldn't be trusted to stay in areas in which they'd remain visible, they'd sleep most of the day, and they'd surely be irritated by the constant boatloads of gawkers and the special effects required to tell the story. The Parks would not get their exotic animal experiences until many years later upon the opening of Disney's Animal Kingdom Park in 1998, when clever, new design techniques enabled separation of animals and people.

The Amazon, Congo, Nile, and Mekong rivers are represented here. The boats, which take their names from these and other rivers of the world, were redesigned in 1998 to effect a more rugged and aged appearance—more in keeping with the spirit of adventure than the relatively pristine boats that had previously circled the river. The spiel, or dialogue, delivered by the skippers has evolved over the years and is constantly being refined.

Lessons learned on Jungle Cruise in the art of landscape design as set decoration have paid dividends in all of the Disney parks. WDI Master Landscape Architect Bill Evans carefully selected a palette of plants that would evoke a tropical feel while remaining hardy enough to withstand the relatively mild (but not tropical) central Florida winters. The plants needed to *feel* correct, even if they would not be found together, or in the types of groupings he used—even on the same continents we portray them to be. Bill broke away from a textbook approach in order to better serve the story.

Harper Goff's early boat concept

QUICK TAKES

• Keep an eye out for a highly appropriate tribute to Bill Evans in the plaza outside the Jungle Cruise queue. The wooden planter boxes in which the large trees are placed are tagged with the fictitious designation "Evans Exotic Plant Exporters." In reality, Bill Evans likely *imported* more exotic plants into this country than anyone else.

• The queue for the Jungle Cruise was reworked in 1994 in order to expand its capacity and provide more shade. Along with this expansion came a corresponding increase in show value, including a substantial propping treatment and the vintage radio broadcast that sets the stage so well for your voyage.

• Look for a great WDI reference in the new propping—Wathel Rogers's name appears on a tag in the animal cage referencing his work in developing the mechanisms for the animals viewed from the boats.

• Check out the crew mess menu posted near the departure point. Hopefully, everybody on this stretch of river likes chicken!

• There's a great bit of wordplay in the name of the Jungle Navigation Co., Ltd. Employee of the Month, seen overhead just before you board. Try saying E. L. O'Fevre fast. And then try not to catch it!

Comedy at First Sight

The art of the WDI sight gag was perfected by Imagineer Marc Davis. His work for Disney Animation, including the classic characters Tinker Bell, Princess Aurora, and Cruella De Vil, gave him the impeccable sense of timing that allowed his creations to read instantly—an important consideration in light of the limited time and dialogue available to us as the audience moves through a scene. His gag sketches for Jungle Cruise were often translated practically verbatim into the attraction.

Disneyodendron eximus
(*Out-of-the-Ordinary Disney Tree*)

How Cool That They Found This Tree Right Here in Florida!

The Swiss Family Treehouse is based on the 1960 Disney film, *Swiss Family Robinson*. This adaptation, based on the 1812 novel by Johann David Wyss (itself a reworking of the Robinson Crusoe story), fit perfectly into our vision of Adventureland. It explores the exploits of a family stranded on a deserted island and their resourcefulness in making a new life for themselves.

A central component of the story is the tree itself, on which the family built their tree house using all the materials on hand, both from the island itself and from the remnants of their shipwreck. Our tree is a bit different, of course, as we have different structural and spatial requirements in our park environment than a family on an island would have. So, Imagineers had to engineer themselves a tree. Ours is based on a banyan tree, a tropical variety that is found in south Florida, that has the convenient habit of putting down vertical roots to support its outlying branches. This gives us the freedom to put down structural supports away from the central trunk, and run them a full 42 feet below the ground for stability.

Our tree is 60 feet tall and 90 feet in diameter. Traverse the 116 steps to get a closer look at the 300,000 leaves. Disneyland's tree, converted into Tarzan's Treehouse® in 2000, is classified (by us) as a *Disneyodendron semperflorens grandis* (large, ever-blooming Disney tree). This makes sense, of course, as it's unlikely that two trees of the same species would be found in such disparate climactic zones. Right?

A Whole New World

The Magic Carpets of Aladdin were added to Adventureland in 2001 as an opportunity to expand on the land in several ways, including physical and thematic. It brought to the Park the very popular characters from the modern classic *Aladdin*, added an entirely new motif to the Adventureland tableau, and provided some much-needed kinetics to the central plaza. The magic lamp of the Genie—discovered, according to the story, when the well at the town center was unearthed—serves as the centerpiece. The addition of the tilt control to the up and down adjustability of the magic carpets already at the control of the Guest, combined with the spurts of water from the camels around the perimeter, makes for a nice plussing of the traditional spinner ride concept.

Don't Tread on Me

The installation of this attraction required significant reworking of the area development in the immediate vicinity. The fountain at the edge of the plaza in front of The Enchanted Tiki Room had to be reduced in order to make room for the ride. It was rebuilt with the help of a mold from the original building construction used for the fabrication of the new backing panels behind the seat wall. The paving now features one of the highest levels of theming in all of the Magic Kingdom. This technique, developed over the years by Imagineering Character Plaster designers, was perfected at Disney's Animal Kingdom and is being introduced to other parks over time as new projects allow. Pay attention to the various treasures embedded in the "dirt" of the city streets. The jewelry is the same as that which you can see being sold in the bazaar or decorating the canopies, and the tiles were taken from a small building that had to be removed in order to make way for the Magic Carpets.

Paving details

Area development plan by Mark Schirmer

Location, Location, Location

The master planning of the individual areas within Adventureland helps us with the transition between Adventureland and Frontierland. The tropical Colonial architecture of the Eastern end works well as an extension of the Victorian flavor of Main Street. The decision to place Caribbean Plaza at the Western end allows us to blend the Spanish-influenced island architecture with the Spanish-influenced Southwestern U.S. architecture of that end of Frontierland as embodied by Pecos Bill's Tall Tale Inn & Cafe. Even the carved wooden facades of central Adventureland work well with the Frontierland pass-through adjacent to

Adventureland as seen from Frontierland

The Enchanted Tiki Room. See how the choice and placement of related styles can avoid a disjointed transition between two lands—even in a case where their settings are worlds apart—and keep the story flowing from land to land.

QUICK TAKES

• The Swiss flag seen over the Swiss Family Treehouse is the only flag of another nation permanently flown over a Disney attraction.

Frontierland as seen from Adventureland

• The landscapers had to bore holes through a solid layer of clay from the site landfill in order to plant the signature trees in the land. The Magic Kingdom site was backfilled to raise the ground level above the pre-existing Florida plain, distancing the Park from the high water table. This also allowed us to build the Utilidor system of tunnels that service the Park from below, well out of the sight of our Guests.

• Many details on the fort over the Pirates entry plaza are based on the Castillo de San Felipe del Morro in San Juan, Puerto Rico, a 400-year-old landmark used by Spanish soldiers to fight pirates centuries ago.

The View from the West

The finials on the roof of The Enchanted Tiki Room tell a great story about dealing with visual intrusion. The building resides entirely within Adventureland, so the South Pacific styling is appropriate. The rooftop, however, is visible from Frontierland, so a choice was made. An Asian water buffalo was used as the basis for the sculpture, with the

intention that from Frontierland the figures would look enough like Western longhorn so that they would not cause a visual intrusion and spoil the view—or the story—from that side. Visual intrusions can be handled in this way as opposed to always being screened off from the areas of the Park for which they are a problem.

You've Got to Maintain Your Standards

These tikis in Adventureland tell the story of the SQS, or Show Quality Standards, program within WDI. This program is the means by which we ensure that the parks maintain their original design intent as they age, grow, and evolve over time. SQS groups work closely with Park operators and maintenance teams to make certain that when any piece of the Park needs to be replaced, it's put back as good, or better. In addition, SQS reviews new designs to align them with existing Park story lines and settings.

Marc Davis's tikis after the addition of the water and steam effects that turn them into a fun piece of interactive Adventure in this playful part of the land.

In the case of these tikis, originally just a piece of area decor, a need to replace the original, wooden figures as they deteriorated became an opportunity to improve upon the concept for future enjoyment. The tikis were rebuilt—this time in fiberglass—with new water and steam elements included for added show. Now they serve as a simple little diversion and a chance to cool off.

45

The Enchanted Tiki Room (Under New Management)

Original Tiki Room concept by John Hench

A Bird of a Different Feather

Our first Audio-Animatronics show at Disneyland in 1963, The Enchanted Tiki Room was often said to have been Walt's favorite. Not bad for an attraction originally conceived as a restaurant—one with a show, of course! After Walt returned from a trip to New Orleans with a little mechanical bird, he became fixated on the idea of improving the mechanism and building a show around singing avians. He first revisited an old Confucius dinner theater concept that had been developed, but never built, for a proposed Chinatown area on Main Street. Eventually he settled on a Tiki backdrop for his singing birds, allowing him to place it into Adventureland. This choice of theming also allowed for the introduction of a huge supporting cast of flowers, masks, drummers, and tikis, all singing along in unison.

The "Under New Management" show at the Magic Kingdom Tiki Room is an example of the WDI practice of "plussing" an idea. By the mid-1990s, after nearly three decades of performances, the Tiki Room show, beloved as it had been, began to feel a bit slow in its pacing. When it was time for WDI to rethink the attraction, and possibly replace it, the significance of the show to our Company's history made the Imagineers reluctant to implement a wholesale change. The decision was made to rejuvenate the production instead, through the introduction of some contemporary comedy and music and a couple of very popular co-hosts. The Enchanted Tiki Room (Under New Management) opened in 1998 with Zazu from *The Lion King* and Iago from *Aladdin* as the two new big birds on the block. The relaxing South Seas tropics have never been the same since!

QUICK TAKES

• The show opened in 1971 and was updated in 1998.

• There are 88 singing birds.

• The voices are performed by:

Iago	Gilbert Gottfried
Zazu	Michael Gough
Fritz	Thurl Ravenscroft
Jose	Wally Boag
Pierre	Jerry Orbach
Michael	Fulton Burley

Iago character concept by Doug Griffith

Real 3-D Animation

The path that led Walt toward Audio-Animatronics began before that mechanical bird. He had been toying around with the idea of mechanical performers for quite some time. One of his early ideas was a collection of animated miniatures called *Disneylandia*—a traveling show of miniatures re-creating moments from American folklore and history.

Walt enjoyed working with his hands, and the animated bird inspired him to improve upon it. As usual, he went into this new enterprise full speed ahead. Soon he had enlisted some of his artists at the Studio. He had Ken Anderson sketching vignettes to be replicated in model form, and Roger Broggie and Wathel Rogers working on the animation technology. All were working in secret and being paid by Walt out of his own pocket.

One of the first scenes attempted was that of a "Dancing Man" in vaudeville showman's guise. With animation modeled after a film of actor/dancer Buddy Ebsen, the crew put their all into making the nine-inch-tall figure move in a lifelike fashion. Eventually, the restrictions imposed by the diminutive size of the scene could not be overcome. The team assured Walt that the results would be more satisfactory if they tried a full-sized figure, which led to the Abraham Lincoln featured at the 1964–1965 New York World's Fair. This is another of the seemingly unrelated events and interests that led Walt, over a number of years, through the evolutionary development of the concept of Disneyland.

47

Street scene illustration by Marc Davis

Fashionably Late

Pirates of the Caribbean at Disneyland was one of the last attractions overseen by Walt, though he did not live to see it open. Originally conceived as a walk-through wax museum in a much smaller space, Walt expanded it and converted it into a water ride after construction was already underway, so that boats could carry Guests through a larger show space.

Pirates of the Caribbean, though declared an instant classic upon its unveiling at Disneyland in 1967, was not part of the Opening Day slate here at the Magic Kingdom. It was thought by the company that Guests in Florida would not be as interested in stories about the Caribbean, due to its relative proximity. But overwhelming Guest requests prevailed, and it made its appearance in 1973. Just as quickly as the original, it became one of the most popular attractions in the park.

There Be Sight Gags Ahead

Much of the charm of Pirates of the Caribbean comes from the ability of WDI designer Marc Davis to create instantly readable sight gags that play into the nature of the world being created. Marc was one of Walt's finest character animators prior to trying his magical hand at the three-dimensional animation that Imagineering considers its stock in trade. This skill, derived from decades of drawing key frames and character designs, informed everything Marc did for WDI. Pirates is full of so many sight gags that it's hard to catch them all on your first voyage.

Gag sketches for Pirates of the Caribbean by Marc Davis

QUICK TAKES

• The name on the coat of arms hanging over the Treasure Room finale scene reads *Marco Daviso*, an obvious reference to the artist and character designer who lent the attraction all of its great sight gags.

• Pirates features the oldest continuously running example of the MAPO Flicker, a special-effects dimmer mimicking the look of a candle or torch. It was developed by Roger Broggie, head of MAPO, WDI's Manufacturing & Production Organization. MAPO also refers to *Mary Poppins*, the film that provided the original funding for the group.

• The Auctioneer is voiced by Paul Frees—the Ghost Host at The Haunted Mansion and the original narrator for The Hall of Presidents.

• Disneyland's Pirates of the Caribbean features two drops rather than WDW's one. While both are required to move Guests out below the Parks' railroad tracks, the Florida version cannot go as deep because of the extremely high water table in the area.

Check, Mate!

The chess game between the two long-gone buccaneers visible from the queue is trapped in a perpetual check. The only available move leads to a never-ending repetition of the same series of moves. One can only imagine how long they found themselves in this state before their untimely demise. Unfortunately, the game was once disturbed during a routine rehab. When it was time to put it back the way it was, none of the Imagineers were able to re-create this oddity and restore these pirates to their ever-so-static state. A search was undertaken to find the notes describing the arrangement. It wasn't until someone looked at the *back* of one of Marc Davis's drawings that they found a detailed sketch laying out the board just as it needed to be arranged in order for the gag to work. Talk about a complicated punch line!

Sketch for the chess-match gag by Marc Davis

FRONTIERLAND

Frontierland celebrates the American pioneer spirit. It is the perfect embodiment of the wonder of the unknown and the quest to discover it, whether it be by land, water, or rail. It's also a time of endless summers and lazy rivers. Stay a while, and you'll see why so many folks choose to call Frontierland "home."

Go West, Young Guests!

Frontierland street scene by Collin Campbell

Frontierland is often referred to as being the most distinctly American statement in all of the Magic Kingdom. It lives as a tribute to the pioneer spirit that drove Americans westward in covered wagons and stagecoaches—a subject that was as near and dear to Walt as Main Street, U.S.A., and equally connected to the fondest memories from his childhood. It's brimming with the excitement of discovery.

The settings of Frontierland represent a time span of roughly 90 years—1790 to 1880. Like Adventureland, Frontierland is made up of several different design motifs, each tied into different bits of American folklore. We see the wooded frontier of Davy Crockett, the Southern banks of the Mighty Mississippi recalling the world of Tom Sawyer, the Southwestern U.S.—identified with the tall tales of Pecos Bill and other American legends represented in the propping inside his Cafe—and Big Thunder Mountain's abandoned ghost town left behind after the Great Gold Rush of 1849.

Frontierland continues a transition in time and location that begins in Liberty Square. You'll notice that even the numbers chosen for the building addresses along this stretch of the Park play into this design direction. The assigned addresses roughly indicate the year in which the building is set, from the 1787 on The Hall of Presidents to the 1867 on the Town Hall of Frontierland. The early-1800s St. Louis styling of the Diamond Horseshoe Saloon at the boundary to Liberty Square marks the end of the East and the beginning of the West—the perfect way for us to head off into the unknown wilderness.

Cold-blast lantern, elevated wooden walkways, and themed area graphics

It's the Little Things That Matter

Frontierland is all about details. The raised wooden sidewalks over the streets of the town are there to keep the mud and dust off boots and dresses of the locals. The flickering cold-blast lanterns, identified by the pipes recirculating air to the top to feed the combustion, help set the date for the land. The posted graphics give us a sense of the time and place of this rustic town. The landscaping is designed to be more natural in appearance than most of the landscaping in the rest of Magic Kingdom Park and is maintained in this less-manicured state. The plant palette even makes use of a type of forced perspective to enhance the feeling of space, bringing the larger species within close proximity of our Guests and placing smaller, closer-planted varieties farther away. This Western-themed land even lies, fittingly, on the western side of our park.

Know Your Subject

Frontierland concept by Sam McKim

Frontierland at each of our Disneyland-style parks features some of the finest atmospheric detailing WDI has done. The set design, propping, character finishes, and landscape all work together to take you there. Inspiration for the design of this land came from the great Hollywood Westerns that Walt and his Imagineers knew and loved so well. These details came from the hands of artists Bill Martin, Sam McKim, and others. Sam had, in fact, gotten his start in the entertainment business as a child actor on the set of many of those films.

Country Bear Jamboree

A WDW Original

The Country Bear Jamboree was the first attraction appearing in both Disneyland and WDW to make its debut in Florida. This Northwoods hoedown at Grizzly Hall is one of the happiest and most energetic shows in all of the Magic Kingdom. It was actually a revision of an idea originally considered for Walt's proposed Mineral King ski resort in California—a stand-alone project studied by WED for several years in the mid-1960s. It is often said that no good idea ever really dies at Imagineering, and Country Bear Jamboree is an excellent example. When the Mineral King project fell through, this Marc Davis concept was reconsidered for use at the Park.

The Country Bears represented a different kind of challenge for our character designers and animators. Unlike Pirates of the Caribbean or The Haunted Mansion, the performers in the Jamboree have to spend significant time onstage in front of an audience, and must remain believable for this longer period of time. The bears, while not needing to look realistic, nonetheless must sustain the illusion of being alive, which tests the capabilities of the Audio-Animatronics system.

The Country Bear Jamboree has proven to be a very versatile production, serving as a great example of the effort Imagineering puts into keeping the parks fresh. Christmas and Summer Vacation shows, introduced in 1984 and 1986 respectively, were developed and rotated in seasonally—with new costumes, new scenic treatments, and, of course, new music themed to these special backdrops. These changes are very popular and extend the appeal of this attraction over the years. Plus, they give the performers a change of pace!

This attraction also shows the power of a song as an anchor to an attraction. When Guests walk out of the theater humming a tune or singing it in their heads, it's a sort of a souvenir. Our show writers absolutely love taking liberties with the lyrics of the well-known and well-loved songs that make up the Country Bears' repertoire.

Big Al

Beloved Big Al in the Country Bear Jamboree is a caricature of Show Writer Al Bertino, one of the lead writers for Magic Kingdom Park. Big Al steals the show every single time he comes on stage.

QUICK TAKES

• The show, which opened in 1971, features 18 bears plus a raccoon, buffalo, stag, moose, and, of course, the occasional skunk.

• Don't miss the claw marks on the floor at Grizzly Hall. The patrons just can't *bear* the wait! This is the fore*bear* of our current techniques of themed paving, adding story to a part of our surroundings we *bear*ly pay attention to.

Back-Country Story

Character sketch by Marc Davis

The story line written during the development of the show tells us the idea was concocted by one Ursus J. Bear after an especially inspiring hibernation season. Ursus then rounded up his musically inclined friends and kinfolk and got to putting on a show. Story treatments like this become the basis for our character designs, influencing the scenic treatment, and determining the specific show content. In many cases in this show, a song was chosen, the lyrics were re-written, and then the bear who would perform it was designed to match the tune.

Sound Tracks

The voice of Henry, our master of ceremonies, is provided by Pete Renaday, a very versatile voice performer. Pete was the voice of Captain Nemo on 20,000 Leagues Under the Sea, and can be heard today as the PA announcer on the Tomorrowland Transit Authority, as well as President Lincoln at The Hall of Presidents.

Our Laughin' Place

Concept sketch by Sam McKim

Splash Mountain, which was added to Frontierland in 1992, is based on the 1946 Disney film *Song of the South*, which in turn was based on characters created by Joel Chandler Harris. That movie, with its mix of live action and animation, related the stories of Brer Rabbit, Brer Fox, and Brer Bear as told by Uncle Remus. Our attraction, a singsong trip through pastoral Southern settings and a big splash down into the briar patch—or laughin' place, depending on your point of view— captures the charm and wonder of those stories. And, Chickapin Hill adds another great silhouette to the skyline of the Park.

The attraction actually came into being during a freeway commute. Imagineer Tony Baxter came up with the concept during one of his long daily drives from near Disneyland to Imagineering in Glendale, as a way to make use of some Audio-Animatronics figures from the America Sings show, which was closing. Imagineers are always thinking about the parks, whether we're on the job or not. When your work is fun you don't mind taking it home!

Story sketches by Don Carson used to plan scenes

Timing Is Everything

Each scene is carefully planned through storyboards and sketches so that it will work in concert with all the others. The flow of each story is worked out just as it would be for a film, with adjustments made for the timing of a theme-park attraction.

Illustration for the finale by Susanne Rattigan

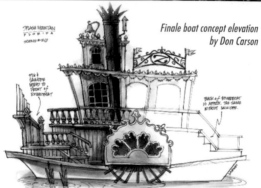

Finale boat concept elevation by Don Carson

QUICK TAKES

• The height of the drop is 52½ feet, at a 45-degree angle, which gives you a speed of 40 miles per hour—faster than Space Mountain!

• The color palette of Splash Mountain's mud banks was shifted from the earthy brown that would have been correct for the Deep South setting to a stronger magenta shade that would work better next to the Western rockwork of Big Thunder Mountain Railroad.

• The runoff after the splashdown is carried into the Rivers of America as a kinetic device and as a way of creating a shared Guest experience. This interaction with the area development allows Guests not on the attraction to see and hear the excitement of those who've just survived the big drop. It's fun both to see and to be seen.

Hats and Glasses, Beware!

The "wildest ride in the wilderness" made its debut in 1980. This attraction took the previously existing genre of the mine car ride and elevated it to a different level. The planning and execution of the environment made it much more than a roller coaster. For example, the rockwork was designed so that it appears to have been there before the 2,780 feet of railroad track were laid, rather than to have grown up around a ride track set into place by theme park designers. This gave it the more naturalistic appearance that is such a big part of the attraction's charm.

The Mountain rises 197 feet in the air, covers two acres of land, and is decorated with lots of authentic antique gold-digging gear—ore cars, lanterns, barrels, tools, and mining equipment such as an old ball mill used to extract gold from ore, and a double-stamp ore crusher. The landscaping of sagebrush and pine helps to complete the setting.

Concept of Big Thunder Mountain queue structure by Sam McKim

A Rock Is a Rock Is a . . . Rock?

The California and Florida Thunder Mountains use different rockwork references. Anaheim's is based on Utah's Bryce Canyon National Park, while WDW's version is based on Monument Valley, also in Utah, but with very distinct characteristics. Bryce Canyon is striated, heavily eroded, and magenta in color. Monument Valley is angular and is rendered in earthy tones. Why was this choice made? Location, location, location. Disneyland's Thunder Mountain lies on the east side of the Rivers of America rather than the west, making it visible from Fantasyland. So, the Bryce rockwork is used as something of a *candy mountain* backdrop. No such visual intrusion exists in Florida. Our intent was for our mountain to carry on the geographic progression from The Haunted Mansion to Big Thunder.

There's More Than One Idea

Early concept sketch by Tony Baxter

Marc Davis used to tell the story of a young designer who excitedly approached Walt in the hall one day to ask what he thought of a drawing the designer had just completed. Walt studied it for a minute, then replied, "I don't know. It's awfully hard to choose between one." The concepts on these pages show how many times we might try before settling in on our "final" idea.

Concept elevation of Big Thunder Mountain Railroad by M. Natsume

Big Thunder Mountain Range ... Mines all mines

Disneyland	Magic Kingdom	Tokyo Disneyland	Disneyland Paris
1979	**1980**	**1983**	**1992**

Frontierland Train Station concept elevation by Don Carson

We're in Training

Splash Mountain was built around the existing WDW Railroad track, while the trains remained in operation at all times. It was a difficult thing to coordinate, but the company feels it's important not to disrupt the show any more than is necessary when we make additions to the Parks. The Splash Mountain project also required the construction of a new Frontierland Train Station to the north of the attraction.

QUICK TAKES

• Hidden in the propping of the Frontierland Train Station, you'll find a wooden leg labeled Smith, a sly reference to one of the silly jokes in the floating tea party scene in *Mary Poppins*. Perhaps you remember it—

> Bert: Speaking of names, I know a man with a wooden leg named Smith.
> Uncle Albert: What's the name of his other leg?

• The Splash Mountain play area under the train trestle is known as the Laughin' Place, and was added in 1997 as a diversion for little tykes who have to wait for family members because they are not yet tall enough to ride the attraction.

• Stand at the Thunder Mountain overlook adjacent to the Rivers of America and enjoy a wonderful Imagineering moment as you view the runaway trains in action. You see kinetics provided by the passing riverboats, trains, and mine cars. You hear sound effects from the ride heard over the area BGM. There are special effects from the steam vents and the geysers to your side, plus themed lighting on the path and theatrical lighting to set the mood on the rockwork. All the elements that make the parks special are wrapped up in one single little vista, just off the beaten path.

Fast Past

At WDI, every project is seen as an opportunity for introducing story into the Park. In the case of the implementation of the FastPass system, begun in 1999, we were challenged with integrating an entirely new queuing system into our existing parks and attractions while meeting all of its operating requirements and not detracting from the existing story lines. This required careful study of each attraction and its particular Guest flow issues, and many, many design iterations. Aside from physical impacts such as potential visual contradictions and traffic impediments, we also had to be certain not to lose sight of any of the various pre-show elements.

In the case of FastPass at Big Thunder Mountain Railroad, this meant bringing the look of the wonderful vintage mining town onto the promenade. We've got dilapidated clapboard siding and makeshift graphics all held up by salvaged railroad ties. There are even signs held up by pieces of leftover rails. These elements are yet another level of detail that helps us to flesh out the Park over time.

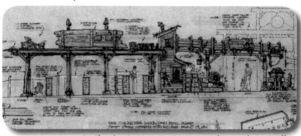

Big Thunder Mountain FastPass station elevation by Jim Heffron

There are always great gags written into the nomenclature on the assorted props and dressings that are placed around our scenes. Pay attention as you make your way around the queue. This crate on the exit side of Big Thunder is labeled Lytum & Hyde Explosives Company.

Height-check sign made from leftover rail pieces

Tom Sawyer Island bird's-eye view by Clem Hall

Oh, to Be Young, Again!

Tom Sawyer Island, the largest playground in all of the Magic Kingdom, recalls a time of carefree youth, adventurous afternoons, and playful memories. It lies in the Rivers of America, an amalgamation of all the great rivers of the United States during the pioneer days. The isolation of the Island from the rest of the Park offers kids a sense of independence, and gives parents a chance to rest in the shade for a while.

The author of "The Adventures of Tom Sawyer," Mark Twain, grew up in Hannibal, Missouri, just about 90 miles east of the town of Marceline, where Walt spent some of the most influential years of his youth. This predisposed the young Walt to a particular fondness for Twain's Tom Sawyer and Huck Finn stories.

The fact that this wondrous place resides on an island required yet another vehicle in order for Guests to gain access. The rafts puttering across the Rivers add kinetics to the landscape of Frontierland and put folks onto a mode of transportation that they don't typically experience. It's also an opportunity to deliver story, as the skipper gives you the lay of the land during the river crossing, and serves as another device to build anticipation, much like the Park entry process, so that your excitement has plenty of opportunity to build as you approach.

The empowerment that children feel in this place where kids rule frees them to explore, daydream, and imagine.

Concept for Ft. Sam Clemens by Sam McKim

The name Ft. Sam Clemens was changed in 1997 to Ft. Langhorne—both references to the author of the source material—to align it with the name of the fort in the Disney film *Tom and Huck*.

A River Runs Around It

The Rivers of America serves as a connection between Liberty Square and Frontierland. It provides us with kinetics, a feature element in the landscape, and a means of isolating Tom Sawyer Island. The Rivers reminds us of a time when rivers were the primary mode of transportation, shipping, and trade, and therefore became home to the majority of settlements. This gives us our setting for the buildings that overlook the Rivers as it winds its way through the Park. Our locations are designed as riverside docks, landings, villages, and outposts. The Rivers provide an evocative backdrop to all the activity that has sprung up around it. It's romantic and inviting and convinces you that something exciting is waiting just around the bend.

Map of the Island to guide our intrepid explorers by Claude Coats

Harper's Mill

Harper Goff is recognized on Tom Sawyer Island with his name on the side of the old mill. The water wheel at this mill once had to be replaced during a rehab. When rebuilt with modern bearings and spindles, it worked too well! A damping system had to be devised to control the speed of the spin and keep it believable as an antique water wheel with rusty parts.

Harper's Mill on Tom Sawyer Island

LIBERTY SQUARE

Liberty Square represents the true spirit of America. It's a journey to bygone days when the ideals of this country were forged. The Founding Fathers would feel right at home. You'll learn a thing or two here, but you'll have so much fun that you won't even mind. Just watch out for that big house up on the hill.

Concept for the land entrance by Herb Ryman

Spirit of '76

Liberty Square is a land that exists only in Magic Kingdom Park, even though it originated from an idea initially suggested for Disneyland. Walt had his designers working on additions to Main Street at Disneyland, to be built off Center Street. The first addition was to have been Edison Square, celebrating the American spirit of innovation. The second was Liberty Square, a walk through Colonial America, reflecting the love of freedom so ingrained in its people.

The choice to include this land in the Opening Day menu in Florida was influenced to some extent by the timing of the Park's debut. Even in 1971, five years ahead of the American Bicentennial celebration, the awareness of that upcoming event had reached a very high level, and made it a popular choice to differentiate Magic Kingdom Park from Disneyland. It's also another link in the chain of Walt's patriotism and the ways it has influenced the Company and the parks.

Another Herb Ryman concept, this time for the land overview

Colonial Style

Liberty Square brings in many elements of Colonial America to lend variety to the architecture. We move from Dutch New Amsterdam (the precursor to modern New York) at the entry from the hub to a Williamsburg Georgian style across the way at Ye Olde Christmas Shoppe. There is the flavor of New England along the waterfront near Fantasyland, encompassing the Columbia Harbour House. Turn toward Frontierland and the buildings become rougher-hewn replicas of structures from the old Northwest Territory.

This street scene by Herb Ryman makes use of period characters in order to set the scene.

QUICK TAKES

• The shutters on the windows hang at an angle, because in Colonial days the upper hinges tended to be made of leather straps in order to conserve metal. This made them list to the side, a quality we mimicked even though ours are made of metal.

• Bricks on the serpentine wall behind Ye Olde Christmas Shoppe came from old buildings being torn down in downtown Orlando.

• The Liberty Bell is a replica cast from the same mold as the original in Philadelphia and was placed there in recognition of the Bicentennial of the U.S. Constitution in 1987. The court of flags surrounding it represents each of the thirteen original colonies.

• The plant palette for the flowering varieties placed into the beds in the land is limited to red, white, and blue.

• The music is all period-specific, and orchestrated to include only instruments that would have been in use at the time.

Hail to the Chiefs

The Hall of Presidents is the cornerstone of Liberty Square. It is a celebration of the leaders who shaped the direction of our nation throughout our history and provides an opportunity to see these great people seemingly living and breathing right before our eyes.

Illustrations for the film by (top to bottom): Ferdi Belan, John De Cuir, and Mike McCracken

You Oughtta Be in Pictures

One of the most ambitious shows developed for the Florida Park, this attraction presented a new set of challenges to the Imagineers. The wide-format illustrations that tell the story of our country's history, presented on a 180° projection screen, beautifully capture some of the most trying and triumphant times our nation has ever seen. Most of the artists assigned to the task of painting these images learned their trade generating motion-picture production art that showed how such scenes could be best represented on film. Typically, however, they did not produce the onscreen image itself. Their unique talents at telling stories through illustrations made them perfectly suited for this task. The stylistic variations derived from so many artists' hands give a richness of texture as well as the drama and the vitality of spirit that the story requires.

Battle scene by Herb Ryman

Illustration for the film by Eddie Martinez

The Hands of a Master

WDI sculptor Blaine Gibson sculpted the faces for each and every president. In fact, he carved nearly every major character figure in the Magic Kingdom and has been brought back out of retirement on several occasions to sculpt important pieces. He is responsible for the pirates in Pirates of the Caribbean, the Country Bears, and the Grim Grinning Ghosts of The Haunted Mansion. Blaine had an

inherent understanding of theme-park attraction timing, which requires that significant story points be communicated in a brief instant. So, Blaine developed the techniques that allow for this quick read. The noses, the eyes, the chins, and the wrinkles are all pushed beyond reality so that expressions are understood, but not so far that the characters cease to appear real enough to carry the story.

Bust of Abraham Lincoln by Blaine Gibson

QUICK TAKES

• The sculpture for the bust of Abraham Lincoln was begun with the use of an actual life mask that was made of the 16th president while he was in office.

• The Lincoln figure is capable of 47 different functions, including 15 head motions and facial expressions.

• Extensive period research was carried out, ensuring historical accuracy in all the costumes and wigs, including textiles, hairstyles, shoe construction, and stitching techniques.

• WDI's first Abraham Lincoln figure debuted at the 1964–1965 New York World's Fair in a show Walt produced for the State of Illinois.

• The date above the door at The Hall of Presidents is the year the Constitution was ratified.

• The Hall of Presidents building is not a replica of any specific building. Rather, it has elements reminiscent of the Federal-style civic buildings of Philadelphia during this time period.

Our Favorite Haunts

Exterior facade elevation by George Jensen

Clearly one of the most popular attractions in the Park, both for the Imagineers and for our Guests, is The Haunted Mansion, which opened in 1971. Who can forget the first time they heard the immortal phrase, "Welcome, foolish mortals?" That first time is practically a *ride* of passage for every young Guest. Our Mansion is a mix of the frightening and the frightfully funny, a balance struck almost as much by accident as by plan. Without Walt to lead the creative effort, two competing points of view developed for the design. Marc Davis, who worked primarily on the characters and gags, wanted a lighter, more playful approach. Claude Coats—a former background painter who focused on settings and atmosphere—favored a darker tone. In the end, Marc's whimsy wins out, but is given life (or afterlife) by the contrast between his gags and the beautiful, darkly rendered environments. Claude had particular influence on the building exterior, where he chose to cheat the wings of the manor toward the front to give the building the stance of an animal readying itself to pounce.

Our Haunted Mansion is based on 19th-century Hudson River Dutch Gothic architecture. This allows it to exist in the hinterlands beyond the bounds of our burgeoning harbor town of Liberty Square. This contrasts with the Antebellum manor in Disneyland's New Orleans Square and the rustic western clapboard house of Phantom Manor in Frontierland in Disneyland Paris.

The Haunted Mansion is the only Disney attraction to appear in a different land in each of the four Parks worldwide. This is a result of varying cultural factors, differing attraction mixes by land, and exciting ideas for a new spin on a classic. It's an interesting testament to the original design, and to the ingenuity of the WDI design teams that found new and different ways to use the venerable Mansion.

QUICK TAKES

• A Guest with good night vision and an affinity for word jumbles may be able to spot tombstones bearing the names of Imagineers who worked on the attraction. *F. Grojere* is for Fred Joerger, Art Director, and *H. Srunb* is Harriet Burns, one of three original members of the WDI Model Shop.

• The wonderful "Grim Grinning Ghosts" theme song was written by X. Atencio, a former animator who got into songwriting only because Walt told him he'd be good at it. In addition to this song and the narration for The Haunted Mansion, X. is also known for his work on "Yo Ho, Yo Ho (A Pirate's Life for Me)" at Pirates of the Caribbean.

• Don't rush by the mausoleum at the exit. There are several great little gags hidden in the names. This type of fun with wordplay is one of the things our show writers like best.

• A rose is often placed in front of the Master Gracey tomb at the entrance. This recognizes the work of Yale Gracey, who led the special effects design team.

Concepts by Marc Davis for a ghostly quintet and the hitchhiking ghosts

Blink and You'll Miss It

The Leota tombstone in the queue area, added in 2001 as an enhancement, shines a spotlight on an Imagineer with a significant connection to The Haunted Mansion. Costumer Leota Toombs, appropriately enough, portrayed the spiritual medium Madame Leota in the séance scene. With this addition, she finally got her due.

Haunting Lands ... The Mansion frightens different neighborhoods worldwide

Disneyland	Magic Kingdom	Tokyo Disneyland	Disneyland Paris
New Orleans Square	**Liberty Square**	**Fantasyland**	**Frontierland**

The Liberty Belle *rounds the bend.*

Riverboat Roundup

The *Liberty Belle* is a landmark at WDW. Often photographed as an icon for the Park, it speaks volumes about the unique nature of the Magic Kingdom and the elements within it. This staple of early frontier life is re-created here, and seen in a setting in which it has not existed in the real world for decades. It offers Guests both young and old an opportunity to experience a bit of our past. Walt felt so strongly about the importance of the Riverboat at Disneyland that when construction funding fell short, he paid for its completion out of his own pocket.

The Riverboat serves as a transitional element linking two lands. Thematically, it works well when viewed from the banks of either Liberty Square or Frontierland, providing all-important kinetics for both lands. The 450-passenger boat was renamed the *Liberty Belle* from the previous *Richard F. Irvine* in 1996 in order to solidify its link to Liberty Square. It had originally been named in honor of the former Vice President and Director of Design for WED, who was instrumental in the design of both Disneyland and Magic Kingdom Park. This steam-powered reproduction was built by the WDW Central Shops.

Riverboat landing elevation by George Jensen

The three storefronts of Ye Olde Christmas Shoppe

Every Fixture Tells a Story

Liberty Square is home to a variety of merchandise locations that beautifully illustrate how WDI uses story to lead design. It's something we do throughout the Park to ensure that storylines are continued in all aspects of the experience. In the case of Ye Olde Christmas Shoppe, designers had a very rich story to draw from. This location, which had previously operated as three distinct storefronts—a perfumerie, a silversmith, and an antiques store—was brought together as a single shop. In order to maintain an individual identity for each space, a back story was devised to give life to each, while tying them together with the unifying theme of the holiday season. One space became the Music Teacher's Shop, decorated with period instruments being prepared for a holiday celebration. Another is now the Woodcarver's Shop—with a more casual, handmade quality—dressed with the tools and materials of the trade, ready to carve Christmas toys. Lastly, we have the home of a Pennsylvania German family, warm and inviting and ready to spread good cheer to friends, neighbors, and travelers alike. This family's name—identified as Kepple—is that of Walt's grandfather, Kepple Disney.

This approach is taken with all our designs for merchandise locations, both interior and exterior. The characters and stories we choose drive the visual design and lend it depth. This can be clearly seen in the design for Madame Leota's Cart near the Riverboat landing, and other outdoor merchandise locations around the Park, as WDI's efforts are not confined to rides and attractions, but extend into each and every bit of show with which a Guest comes into contact during their day.

Design for Mme. Leota's Cart by Mike Kennedy

The lanterns of the Liberty Tree light up as dusk approaches

Let Freedom Ring

The finest natural landmark in all of Liberty Square is the Liberty Tree located across from the entrance to The Hall of Presidents. This tree follows in the tradition of Colonial America by which each town would designate one tree as their symbol of the fight for independence and to serve as the meeting place for the Sons of Liberty. Our Liberty Tree is decorated with thirteen lanterns—one for each of the original colonies.

The Liberty Tree is a live oak (*Quercus virginiana*) that was relocated from the southern part of the WDW property during initial construction. At the time, it was one of the largest trees ever transplanted. Two holes were drilled through the trunk of the tree through which were inserted heavy steel dowels that served as the attachment points for a crane. After replanting, the dowels were removed and replaced by the original wooden plugs. This original wood had become contaminated, however, and the tree developed an illness which threatened its survival. The WED landscapers removed the wooden plugs and the diseased portion of the tree and refilled this space with concrete, allowing the tree to continue to grow. Another smaller live oak was also grafted onto the Liberty Tree at its base to further enhance its appearance.

I Guess It's By Sea

There's a nice little propping detail in the second-floor window on the side of The Hall of Presidents, facing toward The Haunted Mansion. If you look up into this window, you'll see the two lanterns of Paul Revere as described in the famous line, "One if by land, two if by sea."

Westward, Ho!

Liberty Square is the beginning of a very carefully planned aspect of the Park's area development. There is a geographical and chronological transition that sweeps between Liberty Square and Frontierland from The Haunted Mansion to Big Thunder Mountain. This subtle but meaningful design element adds greater depth to the transition between those lands.

We start with The Haunted Mansion, representing New York's Hudson River Valley in the early 1700s. The Columbia Harbour House and surrounding area reflect Boston in the mid-1700s. The Hall of Presidents is, of course, based on Philadelphia of the late 1700s at the time of the Revolution. Then it's on to Goofy's Country Dancin' Jamboree in early-1800s St. Louis, Gateway to the West. Supporting this idea is the little stream that feeds into the Rivers of America at this point—fittingly referred to as the Little Mississippi. Our next stop is the Colorado Rockies and the Country Bear Jamboree's Grizzly Hall in the mid-1800s. As a later addition, Splash Mountain is something of an exception in our travels. Its 1870s-era setting is appropriate, but geographically it forces a detour toward the southern United States, necessitated by the perfect fit of its story into Frontierland. The remainder of Frontierland's shops and restaurants lean toward the pioneer-days styling of the desert Southwest, with a bit of a Spanish flavor. Big Thunder Mountain represents Monument Valley and the end of your journey West.

FANTASYLAND

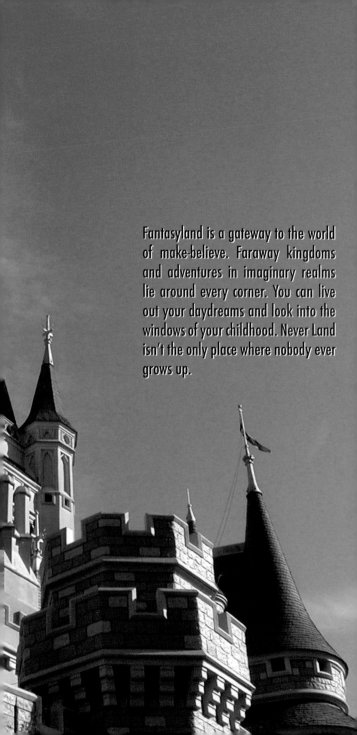

Fantasyland is a gateway to the world of make-believe. Faraway kingdoms and adventures in imaginary realms lie around every corner. You can live out your daydreams and look into the windows of your childhood. Never Land isn't the only place where nobody ever grows up.

Setting the Scene

One Man's Dream

The most magical land of them all is Fantasyland—the heart and soul of the Magic Kingdom. It wraps all of the hopes and dreams of children around the world into the storybook settings they have read about in literature and seen in the fairy tales told in the Disney animated films. Fantasyland is a place of endless enchantment, where it's always "happily ever after."

The setting of Fantasyland is rather eclectic. Inside the Castle walls it's an enchanted European Gothic village. Within resides a pastiche of the various storybook settings found in so much of the source material. There is the medieval tournament-tent look of Mickey's PhilharMagic, Peter Pan's Flight, and "it's a small world"; the Alpine village of Pinocchio's Village Haus; the English Tudor style of Sir Mickey's, Tinker Bell's Treasures, and the Seven Dwarfs' Mine; and the fantastical coastline of Ariel's Grotto. All of these neighborhoods coexist within the walls of the Castle fortress— the common thread being that they are all dressed for festival day, a celebration to which all are invited through the Castle gates.

The seemingly unrelated styles within Fantasyland work perfectly together, owing to their shared message of magic and fun and dreams coming to life.

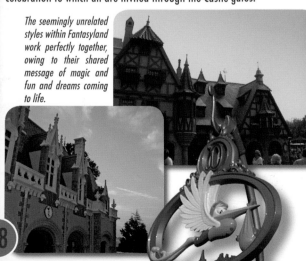

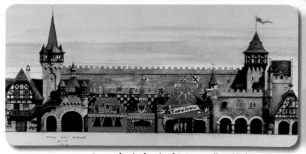

Concept for the facade of "it's a small world" by Herb Ryman

Castles in the Sky

Herb Ryman, consummate WDI artist, is responsible for both Cinderella Castle in WDW and for Sleeping Beauty Castle at Disneyland. In fact, one could say that Herb is largely responsible for the overall look of Fantasyland. It was Herb whom Walt called upon to produce some of the earliest concept artwork to capture the look of this particularly whimsical place. Herbie's architectural knowledge and innate sense of visual communication made it clear that these imaginary worlds could be built in such a way that would make them believable and evoke the essence of the storytelling that Walt wanted to achieve.

You're Surrounded!

As you make your way around Fantasyland, you'll notice hints of details that mimic those of Cinderella Castle peeking out above the rooftops. There are block walls and blue turrets using the same finishes and paint treatments as those on the castle. This serves to reinforce the castle fortress village setting for the land, as demonstrated by the below image taken over Pooh's Thotful Shop.

Change Is Good

The transitions from land to land in our parks are always carefully considered, but the one from Fantasyland to Liberty Square—or Liberty Square to Fantasyland, depending on your point of view—is one of the most successful. This transition takes its cues from the standard film cross-dissolve. In order to make your way from one land to the other, you must pass beneath an overpass, actually a seating area in the Columbia Harbour House. There are elements from each land that appear on each side of the pass-through. You'll see stonework reminiscent of the castle wall in Liberty Square, and Tudor-style woodwork on both sides of the restaurant. Your view narrows and goes dark as you travel through the tunnel, and there is even a separate BGM track playing in this space to complete the dissolve. It's one of the finest and subtlest moments of your walk in the Park.

A Crowning Achievement

The Cinderella fountain, adjacent to Tinker Bell's Treasures across the Castle courtyard, has an interesting little detail built into it.

When viewed from exactly the right angle in front of, and just a little below, the statue, the crown from the background ornament is placed perfectly on Cinderella's head.

Twice as Mice

There are a couple of familiar faces overlooking the proceedings at the receiving line in the lobby at Cinderella's Royal Table. Gus and Jaq from the 1950 film *Cinderella* happily keep tabs on their favorite princess.

A Free Lance Story . . .

The canopy supports in front of "it's a small world" even get the Imagineering treatment. These columns are wrapped in a themed shroud that makes them appear to be medieval jousting lances. This look is in keeping with the tournament-tent motif prevalent throughout the areas of Fantasyland surrounding the Castle courtyard.

Cinderella Castle

Concept to Fantasy

The most striking and most recognizable symbols of all that we do with our Magic Kingdoms are the castles at the center of each Park.

Pencil sketch and concept illustration for Cinderella Castle by Herb Ryman

The design images on these two pages illustrate the highly involved process by which fantastic visions such as the design of Cinderella Castle make the journey from concept to reality–or fantasy, as the case may be. Many steps are required to try out multiple ideas, pin down design details, finalize the architectural requirements, and determine all the colors and finishes that will be applied. Throughout this effort, a project as large and important as the Castle will have dozens of designers adding their own input at various stages of development or reviewing the work of others. WDI is a highly collaborative group, and it is through this shared effort that we are able to achieve results that are more creative than any of us would be able to come up with on our own.

Cinderella Castle differs in several ways from Disneyland's Sleeping Beauty Castle, though both represent the truest example of a Disney Park "weenie." The Disneyland castle owes much of its design to Neuschwanstein–Mad King Ludwig's Bavarian landmark–and stands 75 feet tall. Cinderella Castle uses more French Gothic reference, and a rather more ornamental style that includes elements drawn from various French châteaux such as Chambord, Ussé, and Chenonceau. The Florida castle is also significantly larger, a result of a need to balance with the overall upsizing of the Park. This one is 189 feet tall, much taller than Sleeping Beauty Castle. It's clearly visible from two miles away, as far as the Transportation and Ticket Center.

Castle paint elevation by Debbie Miller

Architectural elevation by Domingos

All Broke Up

The tile mosaic in the Castle breezeway was designed by Dorothea Redmond. It features hundreds of thousands of tiles, including over 500 different colors plus 14k gold and real silver. There were even colors developed for the red rouge of the jealous stepsister and green for the envious one.

The sculpted coat of arms posted over the front and rear entrances to Cinderella Castle is that of the Disney family.

83

Mickey's PhilharMagic concept by Nina Rae Vaughn

A Picture Is Worth a Thousand Words

In the early days of Disney Feature Animation, Walt and his animators instituted a technique of story development that would become a cornerstone of the process. Rather than work from a traditional screenplay, as would be done in a live-action production, they worked from storyboards, a series of sequential sketches illustrating the flow of the action. This approach worked exceptionally well in the visual medium of animation, and has since been adopted as a standard step in the process for almost all forms of filmmaking, especially when the piece has a heavy concentration of visual effects or complicated staging. Imagineering uses storyboards for our own development process, even for attractions without a film element.

This technique was employed during the development process for Mickey's PhilharMagic, which includes one of the most ambitious animated productions ever undertaken for a Disney theme park attraction. The film was a joint effort involving the Theme Park Productions department within WDI working together with Walt Disney Feature Animation. In fact, it was one of Feature Animation's first productions applying CGI (computer-generated imagery) to an entire film—it was the first time they had committed Mickey Mouse and other classic animated characters to this new medium.

Concept by Chris Turner

QUICK TAKE

• Characters can be something other than a full figure or animated face. Donald Duck diving through a wall can be a character if that's what is required to tell a story. At times just a shadow or a voice will suffice.

To Be Continued

The gift shop at the exit of Mickey's PhilharMagic is an example of how our stories can carry on beyond our shows. The set design of the shop makes use of the fact

Donald's frustration continues

that Donald is shot out the back of the theater at the end of the main show. This gives us a hook upon which to hang our shop design. Donald now appears face forward in a tangle of instruments, as though he has penetrated the wall between theater and shop. The motifs of Mickey's PhilharMagic show up throughout the decor. Note the musical notations on the walls and the pieces of musical instruments integrated into the display fixtures.

I wanna be where the people are

I wanna see....

What'ya call 'em

Oh......feet

Mickey's PhilharMagic storyboards by George Scribner

It Was All Started by a Mouse

Mickey's PhilharMagic is an appropriate spiritual successor to the original attraction located in this theater. The Mickey Mouse Revue was a concert performance by lots of favorite Disney characters, led by Mickey Mouse as the conductor, performed here from opening day in 1971 through 1980. It is still playing today at Tokyo Disneyland. Mickey's PhilharMagic is another example of WDI's ongoing efforts to use new technology to tell great stories in new and exciting ways.

Maquettes for Mickey Mouse Revue characters by Blaine Gibson

"it's a small world"

You're a Doll

"it's a small world" debuted at the 1964-1965 New York World's Fair, where Walt presented it as the centerpiece of the pavilion to honor the United Nations Children's Fund (UNICEF). After completing its run at the Fair, it was relocated to Disneyland, and has since been replicated at each of the Magic Kingdom parks worldwide. The WDW version began its run in 1971 with 289 dolls representing six continents and singing the famous song in five languages.

Concept for the UNICEF pavilion by Herb Ryman

Mary Blair Flair

"it's a small world" is one of the purest evocations in three dimensions of the distinctive style of Mary Blair—animator, Imagineer, Disney Legend, and reportedly Walt's favorite artist. Mary's wonderful color studies and background layouts with their childlike innocence made her a perfect fit for the assignment of designing "it's a small world." You may see stylistic links to some of her other prominent work in the films *Alice in Wonderland*, *Peter Pan*, and *The Three Caballeros*.

One of the best known images of the Fair was Rolly Crump's Tower of the Four Winds, seen in this concept elevation by Paul Hartley. This beautiful sculptural mobile was a kinetic icon of the times.

Walt Disney and Mary Blair look over the model for "it's a small world" at WED.

Extreme Makeover, WDI Edition

The WDW version enjoyed a comprehensive restoration in 2005, a focal point of which is the reintroduction of the original 1964 orchestral recording of its beloved theme song. This multitrack stereo master recording, discovered quite recently in a Glendale archive by Imagineer Glenn Barker, reveals the true depth of the composition. The message of hope and wonder is strengthened by the renewed clarity with which one hears the various languages weaving in and out of the mix.

The entry space was also redeveloped in order to link more closely back to the original Disneyland facade. It incorporates the sparkly white-and-gold color scheme, the dimensional set pieces, and of course the classic animated clock which puts on a show every quarter hour.

New entrance area mural created by Jason Grandt for the 2005 renovation

Imagineer and Disney Legend Joyce Carlson has built dolls and costumes for every "it's a small world," including the 1964–1965 New York World's Fair. She's so closely associated with the attraction that when she received her window on Main Street in 1998 it read, "Miss Joyce—Dollmaker for the World."

Cinderella's Golden Carrousel

Horse Trading

Cinderella's Golden Carrousel has one of the longest histories of any of our attractions. It also has a special significance in the history of Disneyland and the Magic Kingdom. When Walt's daughters were young, Saturday was always "Daddy's Day" for him to spend with the girls. One of the places they most commonly frequented was the merry-go-round at Griffith Park, near the Disney Studio. He would sit on a bench watching Diane and Sharon, daydreaming about a place he could go with his family where they could all have fun *together*. Thus was born the idea that led to Disneyland, and all subsequent Disney Parks worldwide.

Cinderella's Golden Carrousel as seen through Cinderella Castle

Old Paint

Our Carrousel's story dates back to 1917, long before the Magic Kingdom was a glimmer in Walt's eye. The Liberty Carousel was manufactured by the Philadelphia Toboggan Company for Palace Gardens in Detroit, Michigan. After a 1928 rehab it moved on to Olympic Park in Maplewood, New Jersey, where it stayed until the park's closing in the mid-1960s. Disney Imagineers discovered it in 1967 while scouting for the new Magic Kingdom under development and rescued it from almost certain demolition. It underwent a painstaking restoration and was in place behind Cinderella Castle when the Park opened in 1971. Its location on that Opening Day was not actually the location of its initial installation in the Magic Kingdom. Roy O. Disney noticed, while on a walk-through of the new park during construction, that the Carrousel was slightly off-center when viewed through the Castle, so he had it moved into place.

Early Carrousel elevation by Dorothea Redmond

The Carrousel's original decor reflected the time of its manufacture. The post–WW I patriotic fervor sweeping the nation led to a red, white, and blue color scheme, and the inclusion of a Lady Liberty figure amongst the horses. Our restoration involved the complete refinishing of all 72 original horses and the addition of several other antique horses purchased from various sources, to bring the total number to 90. In keeping with Walt's insistence at Disneyland, everybody on this Carrousel was to have a horse. And the white horse of a hero or heroine, at that! To that end, four chariots were removed. In order to ensure that any Guest would be able to ride, however, one of the original chariots was added back into the mix during a 1997 renovation, reducing the number of horses to 86.

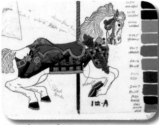

Paint elevation by Kim Irvine

A Horse of a Different Color

Each horse has its own color palette, and no two horses are carved in exactly the same way. Each one has a unique number that can be found stamped into the bridle. The horses toward the outside of the circle are the most

Finished Carrousel horse in place

ornate, as they're the most visible—therefore the most critical to the show.

Each Disney carrousel is different as well. Disneyland's King Arthur Carrousel (which is 3 years younger) is tied into the film *Sleeping Beauty* rather than *Cinderella*. Disneyland Resort Paris has Le Carrousel de Lancelot, adhering more closely to the medieval legends the Park's European setting is famous for. Tokyo Disneyland mimicked the WDW carrousel, but calls it Castle Carrousel and houses it under a different canopy. The one in Hong Kong will be very similar to Anaheim's.

QUICK TAKES

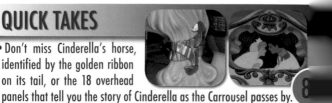

• Don't miss Cinderella's horse, identified by the golden ribbon on its tail, or the 18 overhead panels that tell you the story of Cinderella as the Carrousel passes by.

Peter Pan's Flight

Fly Boy

Who hasn't, at one time or another, dreamed of flying? The answer to that question goes a long way toward explaining the enduring appeal of Peter Pan's Flight. The story of the boy who can fly, from the 1904 play by James Barrie that served as the inspiration for Walt's 1953 film, has captured children's imaginations for more than 100 years.

This attraction indicates the type of thought that goes into the selection of each ride vehicle system. With any attraction, the first step is to try to understand the story you want to tell and the particular *hook* (sorry!) that makes it interesting. For Peter Pan's Flight, we would want to fly through the show. So a system with an overhead track was devised—suspending the vehicle so that it can be carried through the show space as though flying under its own power. This choice dictates the sight lines available to Guests and, therefore, the staging of the show scenes. A designer typically doesn't have to worry about what a set looks like from the top, but in this case, it really matters.

Vehicle concept by Bruce Bushman

QUICK TAKES

• This weather vane, made to look like the pirate ship from the film, brings an element of our show out into our architecture. This detail, and another with the silhouette of the crocodile, adds a touch of whimsy to our Fantasyland skyline. This sort of detail can be placed both above and below your field of vision.

Mr. Smee maquette b
Jack Ferg

• The miniature buildings in the London scene are built in forced perspective, to imply that there is greater distance than there really is between the tops of the buildings and you—and the ground. This heightens the sensation of flying and allows us to vary the apparent height as we move in and out of show scenes. The approach is different than that for the Castle. The models are built with skewed lines that look very odd when viewed from the wrong angle.

It's Dark in Here

Snow White Witch concept by Ken Anderson

Snow White's Scary Adventures is an example of one of our earliest forms for retelling the stories of our classic films, the Fantasyland dark ride. These wonderful little rides move Guests through the world of each film, presenting each story with a charming series of theatrical sets, moving flats, and ingeniously simple effects. The development of this genre was led by Ken Anderson, one of Walt's finest animators, and the art director for *101 Dalmatians*. Ken created the ultraviolet painting technique we use in these shows. It's a mix of both black light and regular white light paint that can be shown under theatrical lighting as well as UV lighting to reveal different nuances of the art as the Guest moves through and the lighting changes. It requires that the artist producing the paint elevations work in a studio illuminated with ultraviolet light, to see the effects take shape. This technique is used to great effect in Snow White to heighten the sense of danger as our heroine makes her way through this scary place.

White light/Black light paint elevations for set walls created by Suzanne Rattigan in a black-light-illuminated office on the Glendale campus at WDI

So, What's in a Name?

The attraction originally focused on the darker elements of the story. Snow White herself did not appear in any of the show scenes, so Guests were placed into her role, to experience her adventures the way she had. For a 1994 makeover, Snow White was added and the attention was drawn away from the Guest, so the word "Scary" was dropped from the title. Soon after the reopening, however, it was returned in order to avoid confusing parents, as the reworking of the show hadn't quite dulled the frightening edge for our littlest Guests.

Mad Tea Party

A New Spin on an Old Story

The Mad Tea Party offers a whimsical take on the 1951 Disney animated classic *Alice in Wonderland*, based on Lewis Carroll's novels. One of the most memorable moments in that film was the zany tea party scene, attended by Alice and her frantic new acquaintances. Imagineers looked for a suitable setting for a pleasant little outdoor diversion, and found it in this scene. The Guest approaches the tea party much the way Alice did. The March Hare's quaint little house is off to the side and houses the attraction's control booth. Japanese tea lanterns add to the festive air of the occasion. The hedges are manicured and the flowers set the scene for the characters depicted in the topiary scene just to the side, inviting you to join in the fun.

The experience captures the madcup—or rather, madcap—nature of Alice's adventures in Wonderland, and one imagines she felt something of the same sense of disorientation by the end of the tea party that we may feel at the end of a few good spins around the floor. This puts the Guest in the middle of the story in an appropriately silly way.

Greenery Scenery

The Disney parks have always been known for their playful topiary statues. These pieces, designed jointly by WDI and WDW Horticulture, are a unique part of our Disney landscape. These pieces can take years to grow, and often incorporate different plants or even other materials in order to clarify the design. The topiaries add set design and storytelling to the environment of the park, while maintaining a pleasant, soft, gardenlike atmosphere. These figures outside the Mad Tea Party even help to draw the show out into the land.

The Alice in Wonderland *characters dance around outside the Mad Tea Party.*

When I See an Elephant Fly

Early Dumbo concept by David Negron

The magic of flight is prevalent in Fantasyland, this time geared toward our little pilots. Often the first attraction visited by a first-time Guest, Dumbo the Flying Elephant is consistently one of the most popular rides in the Park for tots, even though the film on which it was based was released way back in 1941. Dumbo the Flying Elephant was originally developed as a *take off* on the Pink Elephants sequence.

It was decided that this segment of the film might be a bit too scary for small children, so that concept was eventually dropped.

Pink Elephants concept by Bruce Bushman

In 1991, the ride apparatus built for Disneyland Paris was redirected at the last minute to WDW in order to meet an accelerated rehab schedule. This was good for WDW, but the Disneyland Paris team was forced to build a replacement very quickly to be ready for their Opening Day! Our new Dumbo reopened in 1993 with some welcome enhancements. This one features 16 elephants versus the previous 10. The pre-show shade structure and interactive play elements along with a revamped queue featuring topiary animals were added in 1997 as a way to make the wait more comfortable and more enjoyable. Both the Paris and Anaheim versions feature water elements in the center, but Florida's doesn't. Since it is located directly over our underground Utilidor system, the water intrusion issues couldn't be resolved. We already had to bolster the tunnel to handle the additional weight of the new system, while keeping the attraction open at all times!

The Many Adventures of Winnie the Pooh

The Play's the Thing

Storybook concept sketch by Bob Barrett

Some of the most playful stories in all of Disney are those of Winnie the Pooh, set in the Hundred Acre Wood. The world of the Pooh characters is rich and inviting and has enchanted children for as long as a silly old bear can remember. When it was time to replace the venerable Mr. Toad's Wild Ride in Fantasyland, the beloved characters created by A. A. Milne were an obvious choice. In fact, there's an interesting connection between the current and former occupants of this space. In 1929, Mr. Milne produced a play titled "Toad of Toad Hall," based on Kenneth Grahame's *The Wind in the Willows*, the inspiration for Mr. Toad's Wild Ride. There is even a subtle reference to the Toad story left behind in our new Adventure—look at the wall in Owl's House, and try to spot the portrait of Owl and Toad exchanging the Land Deed for the property.

Plan view of The Many Adventures of Winnie the Pooh by Robert Coltrin

Bird's-eye illustration of the Hundred Acre Wood play area by Joe Warren

The Playground's the Thing

The world of the attraction carries over outside the building, into a new play area that was added in 2005. We always try to expand our stories in any way we can, out into the area development of the Park and into additional activities that can be enjoyed. This type of experiential story development is what we consider to be our primary role as Imagineers.

Heffalumps and woozles scene sketch by Don Carson

Scene sketch by Jim Davis

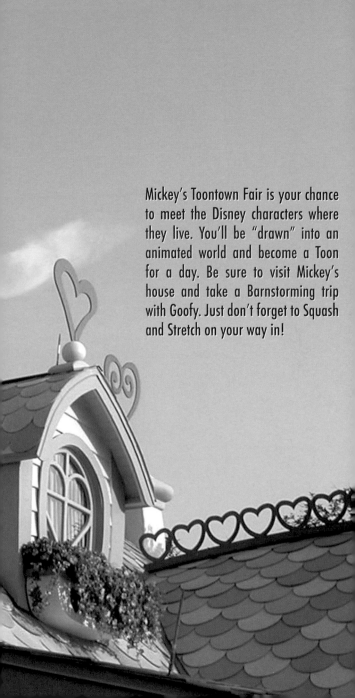

Mickey's Toontown Fair is your chance to meet the Disney characters where they live. You'll be "drawn" into an animated world and become a Toon for a day. Be sure to visit Mickey's house and take a Barnstorming trip with Goofy. Just don't forget to Squash and Stretch on your way in!

Bird's-eye illustration of Mickey's Toontown Fair by Chuck Ballew

Sounds Fair to Me

Mickey's Toontown Fair made its appearance in Magic Kingdom Park in 1996. This land actually began life as Mickey's Birthdayland, installed in recognition of Mickey Mouse's 60th birthday in 1988. It proved such a success that it was quickly converted into Mickey's Starland after the birthday celebration ended. The combination of activities in addition to the opportunity to meet the Disney characters where they live turned out to be such a blue-ribbon winner that the Toontown Fair overlay was developed soon thereafter.

When Imagineers plan a park, they look at all the pieces in terms of how they contribute to the whole. Too much of any one thing wears on us and hinders enjoyment of the story. Families need a variety of experiences to round out their day and to give them periods of excitement alternating with periods of rest. The idea is somewhat akin to the variety that is introduced over the span of a multiple-course meal.

The function of this land within the menu of the Park is clear. It provides some very child-centric activity, and a place for parents to perhaps grab some rest. The magic of seeing these silly and 'toony places, where all of our favorite Disney characters live, brings out the child in all of us. It's a sweet and charming counterpoint to the more active environments found in other places in the Park, much like a film, where the story has peaks and valleys so as not to wear you out before reaching the conclusion. This assortment of sensory experiences is critical to the success of our Parks.

A Different World

The approach to designing for Mickey's Toontown Fair is different from most of our lands, which are based to some extent on real-world times or places. Our direction here comes from the world of Walt Disney's animated short films. If you watch those shorts, however, you'll notice that most of them don't have particularly fanciful backgrounds. Generally, they tend to be somewhat realistic in terms of their architecture and color palette. When we design for our Toontowns, though, we lean toward more playful styling. Why is that? It's because we have a very different dynamic at work in our theme parks versus that of the animated world. In their case, the characters are already 'toony, so the less stylized backdrops ground them and make certain that they remain accessible to the audience. In our case, the streets are populated primarily with real people, so the contrast introduced by the playful surroundings provides the appeal of this make-believe town. Besides, it's more fun to imagine that the characters live in a place like this.

Everything in Toontown is designed with a sense of humor and must support the notion of having fun in a cartoon world. The graphics, the light fixtures, the architecture, and the show sets all play into that. You'll see funny portraits on the walls, wacky color palettes and patterns all around, and a bushelful of sight gags everywhere. Anything that makes for fun is *fair* game. The choice of the Fair motif introduces a built-in level of fun—no matter when you visit Toontown, it's always a special day because the Fair is in town!

Concept by Chuck Ballew for Mickey's Toontown Fair land marquee

Squash and Stretch

Don't Forget to Squash and Stretch on the Way In

The design of Mickey's Toontown Fair makes use of a time-tested technique from the world of Disney animation applied to a different medium—this time a three-dimensional built environment. It's the concept of Squash and Stretch. This is the tool that animators use to give their creations the ability to break the bounds of reality and respond to motion in a way that gives them added life. It's an exaggeration of an action that happens in the real world whereby a mass will compress and then decompress as it goes through a series of motions. This can be seen in a ball that flattens out as it bounces on the ground or in the muscles of a cartoon dog that expand and contract as it runs. Squash and Stretch demonstrates the physics of motion, so that gravity, momentum, and action and reaction are turned into visible forces imparting a cause-and-effect relationship with the character.

As it relates to architecture, Squash and Stretch is expressed in several ways. You'll notice that there are very few straight lines in Mickey's Toontown Fair. Mickey's and Minnie's houses appear to be, though they're not, sort of soft to the touch, like pillows. The props and set pieces—such as the cars, planes, tools, and televisions—all take on a cartoon-y character, almost as though they were inflated from within.

This Squash-and-Stretch approach actually led to some difficulties in getting the buildings built. Construction workers have a tendency to want to make their buildings straight and true, the way people usually want them to be, so we had to work hard with them to get across the notion of how to build a *squashed* house. All those curves were necessary, however, to make Mickey's Toontown Fair a place where the characters could really live. This way, the architecture relates to the characters, and the characters relate to the architecture.

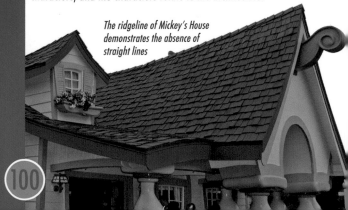

The ridgeline of Mickey's House demonstrates the absence of straight lines

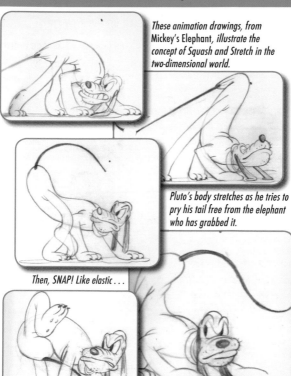

These animation drawings, from *Mickey's Elephant,* illustrate the concept of Squash and Stretch in the two-dimensional world.

Pluto's body stretches as he tries to pry his tail free from the elephant who has grabbed it.

Then, SNAP! Like elastic . . .

. . . the parts squash back into shape!

The Gardener's Cottage in the playground displays the cartoon-y, inflated stance of an animated building. The lines are not straight, and the surfaces demonstrate compound curves that fall along two axes. It's very difficult to manufacture, but just right for our story.

Concept for the Gardener's Cottage by Dave Minichiello

Mickey's and Minnie's Houses

Concept sketches for Mickey's and Minnie's houses by Robert Coltrin

Homes Sweet Homes

The most prominent citizens of Toontown, to be sure, are Mickey and Minnie Mouse. When it comes to designing their homes, located on prime real estate near the heart of town, you have to keep the residents in mind. Each and every element of their houses is designed after their tastes and characteristics. The colors, shapes, and attitudes of each character are used as the stylistic guide for every piece of furniture, each prop, all the decorations on the wall, and the overall architectural treatment of the interiors as well as the exteriors.

Mickey and Minnie like to surround themselves with things that make them feel at home. Notice the cooking utensils, the sporting goods, the games, the lamps, and the clothes. Everything is designed to be a part of their world. These pieces sometimes blur the lines between prop design and show set production, but in the end we always figure out what's what.

Mickey's room concept by Chuck Ballew

Minnie's chair development by Adella Cachu

Concept sketch for Donald's Boat by Robert Coltrin

The Boat's Sprung a Leak!

Imagineers love to play with water, and especially love to find creative ways to get water on our Guests. It can be sprayed, splashed, squirted, dumped, dripped, and dropped, or any combination thereof. Here in sunny Florida, that often comes as a refreshing relief during the course of a long, hot day in the park. Donald's Boat, the *Miss Daisy*, is a great excuse to get everybody wet, and the chaotic nature of the leaky boat plays well into Donald's frenetic personality.

Look closely and you can see that the boat itself is made up of design elements taken directly from Donald himself. The blue of his uniform and the yellow of his bill are both very prominently featured. The roof of the bridge even looks like Donald's cap topping the whole thing off. The entire boat and the experience surrounding it are dimensional representations of the character of our character!

Donald's Boat color elevation by Joe Lanzisero

The Barnstormer at Goofy's Wiseacre Farm

Look, Mom, I'm Flying!

There's something quite wonderful about watching a child enjoying his or her first experience on a roller coaster. The wind in their hair and the smile on their face tells you how new this is to them. It's a big part of the reason we have the Barnstormer here in Mickey's Toontown Fair. The recognizable and comforting face of a well-known character such as Goofy, coupled with the excitement of flying around in cute little airplanes and the playful scenic design, make for a smooth, kid-friendly entrée into the world of thrill attractions.

Paint elevation for Goofy's plane by Vally Mestroni

Concept for Goofy's Barn by Robert Coltrin

Plane Crazy

The design of the plane for Goofy's Barnstormer is pure toon. It's Squashed and Stretched so as to appear fun and comforting to the children for whom it is intended. It's silly and playful and looks exactly the way you'd expect Goofy's plane to look. This approach also applies to the propping and set dressing found throughout the attraction.

Paint elevations for the barn facade by Vally Mestroni

QUICK TAKES

• The chickens you see in the queue were relocated from the World of Motion at *Epcot*® when that attraction was shuttered in 1996. Watch them get flabbergasted as the planes make their way through the barn.

• That jelly-jar lamp in the barn is a silly little play on words. Out in the *real* world, a jelly-jar lamp is a typical industrial lighting fixture with a simple glass enclosure that looks very much like . . . well, a jelly jar. At the Toontown Fair, however, a jelly-jar lamp takes on a more literal meaning. Just a little in-joke from our lighting and prop designers.

The Hall of Fame Tent welcomes Guests entering to meet their friends.

It's a Little *Corn*-y

The Toontown Hall of Fame Tent offers you a glimpse into small-town life here in Mickey's hometown. Out front you see a statue of the town's founder, *Corn*elius Coot. He's standing in the Town Square, on a pile of *corn*, which has rounded *corn*ers, surrounded by growing *corn*stalks. We always like to know the back story of our locales, and Toontown is no exception. It's important to know who lives here, and what their history might be. This is a quaint little town, populated by toons, and it just so happens that the Fair has come to town. One of the highlights of the Fair is the Hall of Fame Tent, where Guests can meet all of their favorite Disney characters.

This is an example of WDI developing a story and designing a venue to meet an operational need. Mickey's Toontown Fair is clearly geared primarily toward our younger Guests, and as such, relies heavily on a character component to make sure that every child gets to meet his or her favorites. This introduces specific functional requirements, which the design has to meet. We have our centerpiece to anchor our Fair motif, and they have a nice, big, comfortable space in which to visit.

Toontown concept art by Dave Minichiello

Cornelius Coot shows off the blue-ribbon crop in the town square in front of the tent.

TOMORROWLAND

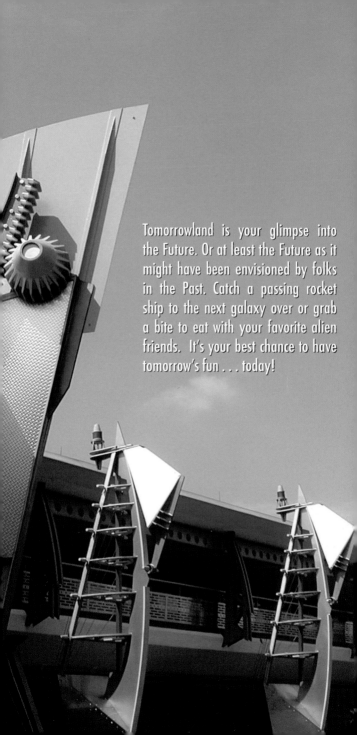

Tomorrowland is your glimpse into the Future. Or at least the Future as it might have been envisioned by folks in the Past. Catch a passing rocket ship to the next galaxy over or grab a bite to eat with your favorite alien friends. It's your best chance to have tomorrow's fun . . . today!

Concept by Tom Gilleon for the entry statement for New Tomorrowland of 1994

In the Future, Change Is Constant

Walt Disney once said, "The only problem with anything of tomorrow is that at the pace we're going right now, tomorrow would catch up with us before we got it built."

It's a fundamental challenge when you build something and call it *Tomorrow*land. There are many different visions of the future that we see in film, on television, in art, and in print. It's one of the most unforgiving subjects on which to give your best guess, because with each passing day we are proving or disproving somebody's vision of the future. But it's just the sort of challenge Imagineers love to tackle.

The first Tomorrowland at Disneyland was barely there on Opening Day. It was intended to be a new and exciting vision of the future (set in 1986), full of optimism and confidence in the abilities that Walt saw in the modern industry of his day. Tomorrowland initially failed to live up to this vision, as its design was clearly a compromise, driven largely by the participation of many partners from the American business community upon whom Walt had depended for funding. As soon as he had a bit more money to work with (from the first few years of operating the Park), Walt set about building ever-grander visions of the future.

The first update of Tomorrowland at Disneyland took place in 1959, and subsequent updates in 1967 and through the mid-1980s continued the effort of staying ahead of the audience's growing expectations. The opening of *Epcot*® with its Future World in 1982 provided the most ambitious endeavor to date.

A Blast from the . . . Future?

When it was time for a New Tomorrowland at Magic Kingdom Park in 1994, Imagineers decided they'd like to build a more fanciful version of tomorrow. A vision of the future rekindled from the past carries with it a charm and a sense of nostalgia that gives it a comforting appeal. Ours is a retro-future concept replete with all the trappings of an intergalactic spaceport. We've got space-age transportation, technology displays at the Interplanetary Science and Convention Centers, and all the comforts and conveniences that science and technology will one day afford us. This design was chosen because it's fun, optimistic, and familiar to all of us, even though we've never really been there. We all remember when we thought the future would be like this. Tomorrowland offers us the opportunity to visit it.

As always, our back story leads our design efforts. New Tomorrowland is conceived as the meeting place of the universe. It's an interplanetary hub chosen to serve as the headquarters of the League of Planets. Everyone who visits Tomorrowland is instantly in touch with the future. When the "locals" need to get somewhere, they hop a ride on the Blueline Express. When anything of note is about to happen, they read about it in the early, early edition of the *Tomorrowland Times*, served up by the robotic newsboy in Rockettower Plaza. Everything in this land relates to excitement and optimism about the future. Every detail relates to this theme. Each pathway leads to a faraway adventure. Pick up a phone and see who answers. Even the palm trees have a technological bent!

New Tomorrowland poster demonstrates the fantastic vision of the bustling intergalactic gathering place Imagineers envisioned.

Walt believed that the solutions to many of our problems would lie in our ingenuity and thoughtful design. Imagineers are generally very optimistic types as well, and they share Walt's fascination with the future. That's why we keep trying to design it!

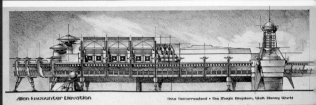

Alien Encounter Elevation

New Tomorrowland • The Magic Kingdom, Walt Disney World

Moving Right Along

Tomorrowland has always been our "land on the move." It has a palpable kinetic energy imparted by the PeopleMover gliding around the perimeter, the star field and rockets of the Astro Orbiter whirring by overhead, the race cars of the Tomorrowland Indy Speedway whizzing past, and even a building itself spinning in place over at Carousel of Progress. This type of activity is important to all of our lands, but especially to Tomorrowland, which we all want to see as a fantastical vision of technology and progress. The implication, however subconscious, is that the world, and the galaxy, and the universe itself will become smaller and more accessible to us as our transportation systems advance.

Details, Details, Details . . .

Take a good look at all of the finishes, materials, design detailing, and surface treatments throughout Tomorrowland. There are brushed metals, cast-steel machine parts in the attachments, and otherworldly materials and patterns poured into the paving. Each was carefully conceived and thoughtfully executed so as to add layer after layer to the scenic design of Tomorrowland. We can believe that we're walking around a futuristic metropolis and bustling spaceport, because we support that story with every little thing we put into the land.

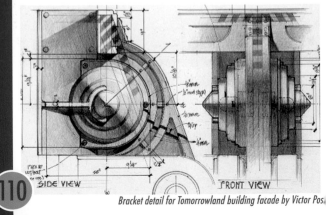

Bracket detail for Tomorrowland building facade by Victor Pos

Circle-Vision/Delta Dreamflight Elevation — New Tomorrowland • The Magic Kingdom, Walt Disney World

Architectural facade elevations for New Tomorrowland by Gil Keppler

Note that the paving in Tomorrowland is yet another element that adds to the design intent of the land. The new treatment, which was implemented with the 1994 New Tomorrowland update, features lines drawn from orbital paths and planetary shapes much like those found on the Astro Orbiter. The paving is also comprised of a mix of materials, such as concrete in various colors with varying degrees of sandblasting to expose the aggregate, plus embedded stones and other accent pieces. This materials palette was chosen to complement the materials that appear on the architecture in the area, while expanding the story in another direction.

A nighttime view down the central corridor of New Tomorrowland

Let's Shed Some Light on the Subject

Often the task of the lighting designer goes beyond casting light onto buildings or show elements. Sometimes the design of a scene requires the lighting to be an integral part of the architectural design. Tomorrowland, perhaps more than any other land, gains a special energy when the sun goes down and the lights go on. The strip lighting, neon, and facade lighting are important devices in suggesting our "retro" future.

Tomorrowland Transit Authority

Concept by George McGinnis for the WEDway, the centerpiece of the "land on the move"

Moving People Toward the Future

The Tomorrowland Transit Authority (TTA) is a key component of our "land on the move." It's the primary means of commuting from the hoverburbs outside Tomorrowland. Walt believed that the future would be a vibrant time, with innovations just around the corner, each holding the promise of bettering our lives. Transportation was a big part of this thinking, as he looked for ways to solve the problems of our cities. A system with the capability to move large numbers of people around crowded city centers without interfering with existing traffic patterns or generating additional pollution would be of tremendous benefit.

The first concept came at Disneyland in 1967 during the second major overhaul of Tomorrowland. It differed from WDW's—originally dubbed the WEDway in recognition of Walt's fondness for such inventiveness— in its technology but not in its mission. Disneyland's (since removed) featured a series of tires set into the track, continuously driven by electric motors, upon which the trains were carried, with no moving parts of their own. The varying speeds of the tires and the moving walkway at the load platforms enabled riders to board the vehicle without it having to stop. By the time the second iteration was installed at Magic Kingdom Park in 1975, there were new technologies available which allowed us to plus the concept. This time, the tires in the track were replaced by 533 electromagnets generating an effect called linear induction. These magnets, with a carefully timed sequence of pulses, are able to push and pull the train around its 4,574-foot circuit, again without any onboard moving parts.

Sneak Peek

The TTA is a great way to get a preview of all there is to see in Tomorrowland. The system was carefully integrated with all the other venues in the land to heighten the interaction between all the elements. This adds to the kinetics, from both sides of the glass.

Early concept for the PeopleMover produced by George McGinnis during design development in 1969

Way Outside the Berm

There is, in fact, one real-world application of the PeopleMover technology implemented by the Imagineers. It is a system installed at the Houston Intercontinental Airport in 1981, for which the Disney company consulted. That train uses the same linear induction propulsion system to move, but the vehicles are different in order to accommodate the specific traffic requirements of the airport.

Backdrop to Walt's 1963 EPCOT model by Herb Ryman

Model Citizens

Be sure to pay attention to the large model you see at track left on your way through the first tunnel. This is a portion of the original Progress City model for EPCOT (Experimental Prototype Community of Tomorrow) conceived as the centerpiece of Walt's Florida Project. The original concept for EPCOT was a complete living and working city, serving as an example for future urban development. The legacy of this concept can be seen in such subsequent Imagineering efforts as the *Epcot*® theme park, the master-planning of the WDW property, and the Celebration town project.

QUICK TAKE

• The page for Mr. Tom Morrow is a WDI inside joke. This refers back to the head of operations at Mission to Mars, which used to lie along the TTA track. It also connects us forward to *Epcot*®, where Tom Morrow 2.0 serves as host of Innoventions.

Stitch's Great Escape

Storyboard art by Chris Turner demonstrates the sequence of action for Stitch's Great Escape.

A Stitch, in Time

Magic Kingdom Park is the place where our classic Disney characters live. It's rare for a character to take up residence here just three years after his first appearance, but the little blue alien, Stitch, was clearly an instant classic. From the time he made his animated debut in the film *Lilo & Stitch* in the summer of 2001, it was only a matter of time before he arrived on the scene in Tomorrowland.

Translating a two-dimensional character into three dimensions is always challenging, especially when the central figure is as distinctive as Stitch. So, the attraction makes use of almost all of our senses to express his unique personality in many different ways—notably demonstrating the power of audio as a storytelling medium. The use of a binaural (stereoscopic) sound system dedicated to each seat allows Stitch to *appear* to be on any side of the Guest, as the story requires. This is accomplished by varying the audio mix from one ear to the other in order to replicate the spatial positioning we perceive in the real world. When combined with Audio-Animatronics, set design, lighting, on-screen animation, and special effects (including scent), a truly immersive theatrical environment is created.

The development of this attraction made use of new design and production processes available to us with the advent of digital technology. These include digital paint on the storyboards, CGI concepts, and digital rapid prototyping for specialty manufacturing. Onstage and off, Imagineers always look for new and better tools with which to tell our stories.

Digital concept art for the Hotwire Effect by Doug Griffith

Going Through the Motions

Pre-visualization art by Rick Daffern

Storyboards guided the development of this pre-visualization model, which, in turn, was used to determine the timing of the show and the audience sight lines. This dictated the proper staging of the figure and helped determine the specific functions that were required. Those criteria then led the design development of the figure. This one was particularly difficult due to his very specific physiology—large head, skinny neck, big, expressive ears, and rapid-fire movement. This coupled with his proximity to the audience, 360° of visibility, and the duration of his time on stage definitely raised the stakes on this performance. Stitch, with 48 functions packed into a 39-inch-tall frame, and the ability to "walk" around, is one of the most complex figures ever created by WDI, taking his place in a lineage of milestone figures, along with Abraham Lincoln, Ben Franklin, the Wicked Witch, and Hopper.

Animation sketches by John Cutry

The WDI animator often does sketches of the poses the character should strike along the way, much like the key frames drawn by the animator of a film character. It's essential that the animator have a complete understanding of the capabilities of the figure before taking it into the field for its final programming.

This Space's Time(line) Continuum

Flight to the Moon	**1971-1975**
Mission to Mars	**1975-1993**
The ExtraTERRORestrial Alien Encounter	**1995-2003**
Stitch's Great Escape	**2004-????**

Tomorrowland Indy Speedway

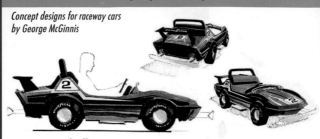

*Concept designs for raceway cars
by George McGinnis*

License to Thrill

What little kid doesn't want to drive a car? What big kid doesn't want to drive a race car? Those questions reveal the heart of the Tomorrowland Indy Speedway. Formerly known as the Grand Prix Raceway, this 2,260-foot Tomorrowland staple has been offering a first driving experience to generations of young Guests.

The Tomorrowland Indy Speedway is a modern interpretation of the classic Disneyland Autopia. When Disneyland opened, the interstate highway system was just being implemented. In keeping with his long-standing interest in education, Walt felt that Autopia could go a long way toward teaching kids how to drive on the new roadways. The original Autopia featured no guide rails, so the cars were constantly bumping into each other as they made their way around. Guide rails were, of course, quickly added to keep everybody on track. Unfortunately, however, similar rails have still not made it to the Los Angeles freeways.

Freeways were a routine part of everyday life by the time the WDW version was built in 1971, so a new theme was devised, placing the Guest on a high-speed (7.5 mph, anyway) racetrack of the future. The design of the cars is a model of timeless form. While the graphics applications have changed occasionally over the years, the shape still manages to look fresh and contemporary.

Concept by George McGinnis for the Florida update of Autopia.

Computer-generated model by Michael Browne

Paint elevation by Vally Mestroni

Concept by Steve Anderson for the redesign of StarJets for New Tomorrowland.

Let's Go for a Spin

One of the primary contributors to the kinetics of Tomorrowland is the Astro Orbiter. This attraction, a plussing of the original StarJets, took on its current appearance in the New Tomorrowland redesign of 1994. This spinning ride gets a particular level of thrill not just by way of the obvious—its elevated height—but also from the context given by the proximity of the various planets and moons spinning about *you* as *you* spin about them. Were you to fly around at the same height but without the planets (as in the original StarJets) you wouldn't have quite the same sensation of speed that you get now. It's much like the way your trip down the highway feels slower without buildings, signs, or trees nearby to signal your progress.

The Astro Orbiter actually only spins at about 11 revolutions per minute, but you'd swear you were doing at least a couple of times the speed of light . . . give or take. It's one of the best ways to get a bird's-eye view of Tomorrowland, and another entry in the intriguing set of transportation options that makes Tomorrowland feel truly out of this world.

| **12** vehicles | **40'** radius of arm | **11** RPM | **1.2** million miles per year |

Space Mountain

The first concept sketch of Space Mountain, by John Hench, 1965

A Rocket to the Future

Space Mountain is one of the truly classic Disney attractions. One of the first major E-Ticket attractions to make its debut in Walt Disney World rather than at Disneyland—in December 1974—it was a fairly radical idea when introduced. No one had tried placing a roller coaster inside a darkened building before, but it was a necessary part of the story. We needed to have the control over lighting offered by being inside in order to convince a rider that he or she is hurtling through outer space, and we didn't want a typical, exposed roller-coaster track to spoil the other stories we were telling in the surrounding area.

Space Mountain captures the spirit of its era, when the exuberance of the race for space had taken hold around the world (literally and figuratively). It was a time of great imagination regarding what awaited us out there. Space Mountain offers up a playful vision of a time when a trip around the planet might be as casual and recreational as a typical Sunday drive.

Early concept by George McGinnis for the classic Space Mountain rocket ship

QUICK TAKES

• It is *not* true that the large meteorite with the many craters passing overhead is actually a photo of a chocolate-chip cookie.

• The mountain is 183 feet tall, and the spaceships travel at a top speed of 28.7 mph.

Concept for the building exterior by Clem Hall

The unmistakable silhouette of Space Mountain

Beaming on the Outside

A key contribution to the distinctive look of Space Mountain came from John Hench when he saw the first schematic drawings that called for concrete beams to hold up the roof structure. Typical construction techniques would call for those beams to be placed on the inside of the building, with the roof surface applied on the outside. John insisted that those beams be put on the outside, for two reasons: it allowed for a smooth surface on the inside onto which the star field and meteors could be clearly projected, and also created a bit of forced perspective on the exterior as the columns converged toward the top of the building, increasing the apparent height of the structure. This look, designed over thirty years ago, still works as an image of the future, as it falls well outside the norm of what we tend to see during our day-to-day lives.

Space Mountain Range... Blasting off around the world

Magic Kingdom	Disneyland	Tokyo Disneyland	Disneyland Paris	Hong Kong Disneyland
1974	1977	1983	1995	2005

Buzz Lightyear's Space Ranger Spin

Concept by Chuck Ballew for Buzz Lightyear's Space Ranger Spin

Round and Round and Round

Whenever Imagineering considers a new attraction for development, a good story is always the first piece of the puzzle. Buzz Lightyear's Space Ranger Spin, opened in 1998 in the space formerly occupied by If You Had Wings, takes us into the story-within-a-story from the two *Toy Story* films—the Gamma Quadrant as patrolled by the "real" Buzz Lightyear. We join forces with Buzz as he battles Evil Emperor Zurg in his efforts to steal the batteries used to power the toys.

Once the story is set, it often leads us toward the proper format through which that story should be told. In the case of Space Ranger Spin, the answer was to take our inspiration from the world of modern video games, leading to one of our most interactive attractions. Of course, we wanted to make that genre function in a way that turns it into a group activity for the whole family to enjoy together. This whimsical, colorful, shooting-gallery-on-a-track allows Guests to influence the show. Interactivity to this extent is a rather new development in the world of theme-parks. People feel more engaged with the story when it works both ways. Besides, it's just plain fun!

In developing this attraction, Imagineers made use of the traditional continuous-motion OmniMover system—like the one you'll find in The Haunted Mansion—in a new way. We added the capability for the vehicle to spin a full 360°, entirely at the control of the Guest, while remaining in forward motion through the show scenes all the time. The engineering effort required to package that capability into a pre-existing ride system was a remarkable feat. The show control system communicates with each vehicle continuously, and keeps track of each blaster's hits and scores in order to give players their rank upon exiting.

Ride vehicle concept by Chuck Ballew

Double Take

These two concepts, for the ride vehicle and the blasters, show how similar our initial designs can be at times to the finished piece. Sometimes designs change in process, sometimes not.

Blaster concept by Chuck Ballew

Previous Tenants . . . Each of these attractions has made its residence here.

If You Had Wings - June 5, 1972 through June 1, 1987

If You Could Fly - June 6, 1987 through January 3, 1989

Delta Dreamflight - June 26, 1989 through December 31, 1995

Take Flight - January 1, 1996 through January 5, 1998

Buzz Lightyear's Space Ranger Spin - October 7, 1998 to Infinity . . . and Beyond!!!

Carousel of Progress

The finale scene of the Carousel of Progress as rendered by John Hench

Taking a Turn for the Better

Perhaps no single attraction in all of our parks more clearly bears the signature of Walt Disney than the Carousel of Progress, which began as the centerpiece of the General Electric exhibit at the 1964–1965 New York World's Fair. It's even on the marquee. Walt's appreciation for nostalgic recollections of American life are combined with his true vision for a brighter future through innovation to create a loving tribute to the enterprise of those who have brought to us all the conveniences of modern life. Whatever modern means to you, that is. The show follows four generations of a typical American family as they experience the wondrous changes we've experienced in our typical day-to-day lives, primarily through the advent and development of electrical products.

Concept sketch by Marc Davis for the 1890s scene

Show design illustration for a future scene by Collin Campbell

Spin Cycle

The Carousel of Progress is quite likely the single most frequently performed show in the long history of American theater. It has run more or less continuously since 1964. It's enough to make a theater dizzy!

Concept sketch for the 1920s scene by Marc Davis

Theme Song

The theme song to Carousel of Progress has always been closely identified with the show. The thing is, it hasn't always been the same theme song! A song titled "There's a Great Big Beautiful Tomorrow" was created for the original show at the World's Fair. This song remained in place during the Carousel's subsequent stay at Disneyland. When it was relocated to WDW in 1975, the song was changed. The new one was entitled "The Best Time of Your Life." The two songs are variations on a theme, both embodying the overriding idea of progress exemplified by the show. In 1996, the attraction was updated to reflect Walt Disney's original vision, and with that change, the original theme song was restored.

The Brothers Grin

The aforementioned theme songs were both written by the Sherman brothers—Richard M. Sherman and Robert B. Sherman—longtime collaborators with Walt Disney. These two songwriters have written songs for Disney films and theme park attractions from *The Jungle Book* to *Mary Poppins* to Journey into Imagination at *Epcot®*. Their ability to turn a phrase and tell a story through song made "The Boys" real go-to men for Walt.

QUICK TAKES

• The dogs have gone by many names over the years—at various times Rover, Sport, Buster, and Queenie. As of 1994, they're all Rover.

• The 1920s scene can be traced to 1927. Listen for the Charles Lindbergh reference on the radio broadcast.

• The current voice for the Grandfather, Rex Allen, was the voice of the father in the original New York World's Fair recording.

The Timekeeper and Nine-Eye survey the span of history in this concept by George Stokes

There's Always a Bigger Idea

Another example of the Imagineering tendency toward plussing ideas is The Timekeeper, set at the Interplanetary Convention Center. This attraction, which debuted in November 1994, takes the classic WED invention of the Circle-Vision theater and goes it one better by adding characters and effects into the space to go along with the nine projection screens that surround the space and engulf the viewer in the scene.

The idea for Circle-Vision, originally dubbed Circarama, came to Walt when he saw a Cinerama presentation at a theater in Hollywood. He came back to the studio and asked Roger Broggie why, if they could put three screens together, they couldn't go all the way around. Broggie and his team—which included longtime Disney associate Ub Iwerks, a self-taught expert on optics—were able to present Walt with a workable system after much experimentation. This system made its debut at Disneyland on Opening Day in 1955. It has thrilled audiences over the years with enveloping imagery typically celebrating the beauty of the American landscape, both urban and natural. Circle-Vision shoots are very complex to coordinate, as each 360-degree view needs to be clear of any element that would throw you out of the scene. A Circle-Vision theater always has to have an odd number of screens, so that each image can be projected from a blank spot between the screens directly opposite it around the circle.

The Timekeeper and its sister attraction Le Visionarium, formerly at Disneyland Paris, mark the first attempts to use the system to deliver a narrative story line. This required a conceit to explain the unusual visual characteristics of the theater, hence the character Nine-Eye. Nine-Eye is sent through time by The Timekeeper, so that she can send back the surrounding images as she records them in whichever era she finds herself.

Set the Show

An interior sketch by James Wong leads the show set design

Examples of Show Set Design are readily accessible here in the lobby of the Convention Center. Observe the way the architectural elements from the show are expressed in big and small details throughout the space. This design effort takes off from concept sketches and gets into a level of detail that can only be achieved through a rigorous development process. You have to think about how every detail would be handled within the world in which this attraction is set. It must relate to the show in the main theater, to the architectural facade that you pass through on your way in, and to the area development of the land overall. All pieces must fit properly into the whole.

Through this process, the Show Set Designer takes the concept design drawings, which are often somewhat loose and evocative, and interprets them, with help from an art director, into buildable elements accounted for in the overall planning of the production. The architects must know your requirements for set locations, the engineers have to know what sort of structure to provide, and park operations needs to know how much space is left for Guest flow. These considerations, among others, ensure that the whole experience works together.

Finished theater lobby

We hope you've enjoyed this tour of the Magic Kingdom as much as we have. Now you can see the Park through the eyes of an Imagineer. Look for these and so many other little gems hidden in plain sight all throughout the Park. Take in all the stories and all of the richness of detail that we've had so much fun putting there for you. But most of all, we hope you . . .

Enjoy the Park!

BIBLIOGRAPHY

The Art of Walt Disney, Christopher Finch, Harry N. Abrams, Inc., 1973, rev. 1995, 2004

A Brush with Disney—An Artist's Journey, told through the words and works of Herbert Dickens Ryman, edited by Bruce Gordon and David Mumford, Camphor Tree Publishers, 2000

Building a Dream: The Art of Disney Architecture, Beth Dunlop, Harry N. Abrams, Inc., 1996

Designing Disney: Imagineering and the Art of the Show, John Hench with Peggy Van Pelt, Disney Editions, 2003

Designing Disney's Theme Parks: The Architecture of Reassurance, Karal Ann Marling, Flammarion/CCA, 1997

Disney A to Z: The Official Encyclopedia, Dave Smith, Hyperion, 1996, rev. 1998, 2005

Disney: The First 100 Years, Dave Smith and Steven Clark, Hyperion, 1999, rev. 2002

Disneyland, Martin A. Sklar, Walt Disney Productions, 1963

Disneyland: Dreams, Traditions and Transitions, Leonard Shannon, Disney's Kingdom Editions, 1994

Disneyland: The Inside Story, Randy Bright, Harry N. Abrams, Inc., 1987

Disneyland: The Nickel Tour, David Mumford and Bruce Gordon, Camphor Tree Publishers, 1995

Remembering Walt: Favorite Memories of Walt Disney, Amy Boothe Green and Howard E. Green, Disney Editions, 1999

Since the World Began, Jeff Kurtti, Hyperion, 1996

The Story of Walt Disney World, Walt Disney Productions, 1978

The Haunted Mansion: From the Magic Kingdom to the Movies, Jason Surrell, Disney Editions, 2003

Walt Disney Imagineering: A Behind the Dreams Look at Making the Magic Real, The Imagineers, Hyperion, 1996

Walt Disney World: 20 Magical Years, The Walt Disney Company, 1991

Walt's Time: From Before to Beyond, Robert B. Sherman and Richard M. Sherman, Camphor Tree Publishers, 1998